Southern
SMOKE

Brimming with creative inspiration, how-to projects, and useful information to enrich your everyday life, Quarto Knows is a favorite destination for those pursuing their interests and passions. Visit our site and dig deeper with our books into your area of interest: Quarto Creates, Quarto Cooks, Quarto Homes, Quarto Lives, Quarto Drives, Quarto Explores, Quarto Gifts, or Quarto Kids.

First Published in 2019 by The Harvard Common Press, an imprint of The Quarto Group,
100 Cummings Center, Suite 265-D, Beverly, MA 01915, USA.
T (978) 282-9590 F (978) 283-2742 QuartoKnows.com

The Harvard Common Press titles are also available at discount for retail, wholesale, promotional, and bulk purchase. For details, contact the Special Sales Manager by email at specialsales@quarto.com or by mail at The Quarto Group, Attn: Special Sales Manager, 100 Cummings Center, Suite 265-D, Beverly, MA 01915, USA.

23 22 21 20 19   1 2 3 4 5

ISBN: 978-0-7603-6402-4
Digital edition published in 2019

Library of Congress Cataloging-in-Publication Data available

Design: Landers Miller Design
Cover Image: Felicia Perry Trujillo
Page Layout: Megan Jones Design
Photography: Felicia Perry Trujillo
Illustration: Shutterstock

Printed in China

Southern SMOKE

BARBECUE, TRADITIONS, AND TREASURED RECIPES
REIMAGINED FOR TODAY

Matthew Register

HARVARD
COMMON
PRESS

CONTENTS

FOREWORD

At Crook's Corner, we've been hosting a "guest barbecue night" for years. Every Wednesday, we invite pit masters to join us or send us some of their barbecue. Since barbecue is contentious here in North Carolina, like college basketball, we try to include restaurants from both the east and the west of the state in equal measure. Often, when Matthew sent us barbecue, he would also send one of his side dishes. The one that made me decide I needed to go from knowing of Matthew to meeting him was his collard chowder. It stopped me in my tracks. "How come I've never heard of this?" I asked myself. "It is so delicious. I need to know this guy . . ."

We finally did meet when Matthew and his sidekick, Rodolfo Sandoval, delivered a shipment in person. I immediately loved his point of view: the way he views his cooking and the way it informs how he lives his life. If that's hard to understand, just start reading. His philosophy comes through clearly in the pages of this book. He wants his guests to have a good time first of all, and he thinks that they should do that with good friends and food. (And it is really good food.)

Matthew's restaurant kitchen, over in Garland, North Carolina, is tiny. You could spit across it, as my grandmother would have said, except that it would get in trouble with the health department if you did. I know this as I had the honor and the pleasure of being a guest chef at one of his

Southern Supper Series events a few years back. His place at that time was mostly for takeout with a few picnic tables out front. But off to one side was a nice covered area that can seat a party and there was a food truck in the driveway. Best of all, there was a 1965 Ford that had been turned into a bar in the back. We climbed all over each other as we worked in the little kitchen, and that night a crowd gathered for supper. Matthew's family was all there—mostly as workers—as were Rodolfo's parents. Some local farmers and other neighbors stopped by. Rounding it out were food enthusiasts from further afield, who had discovered Matthew's dinner parties. The menu included some of my food and some of his. It was a grand evening.

Because I'm in a restaurant kitchen eighty hours a week, I never cook at home; if I did, I would use the recipes in this book to recreate some of what we cooked that night and to make my own barbecue (dream on). I'd then follow Matthew on wonderful tangents: smoked turkey, all kinds of chicken, fried oysters—all the things you might expect to find in a cool Southern barbecue shack. The collard chowder I remember so well is here. So are Merigold tomatoes, another recipe that made me want to meet this chef.

Matthew means for you to really use this book. He starts with the elemental, like in the Joy of Cooking, where they tell you how to boil water.

For barbecue, that means he covers what kind of wood, temperatures, equipment, even the fun factor. No stone is left unturned.

After addressing our North Carolina barbecue and its embellishments in depth, he explores a few other regional cuisines of the South. First to the Low Country, with its sophisticated food traditions, and then to Memphis and the Delta region of Mississippi that adjoins it—favorite places of mine. Along the way are stories, opinions, and bits of history. Some of the recipes stick close to tradition, while others have been altered a little to suit modern tastes and times.

Finally, there is a splendid section on baking and desserts. If you'll pardon me, this takes the cake. Besides standards like black pepper cornbread and buttermilk biscuits, you get your pick of pies: chocolate chess with pecans, sweet potato, buttermilk, coconut cream, peanut, chocolate fudge with sea salt, and then something called pecan pie bread pudding. He doesn't mess around.

You're going to love this cookbook . . . just make sure you try that collard chowder.

—**Bill Smith, Chef, Crook's Corner, Chapel Hill, and author of** *Seasoned in the South*

INTRODUCTION

I didn't set out to become a chef. In fact, even once cooking all day was my full-time job, I was uncomfortable with the title. I didn't have a family lineage tracing back generations in the restaurant business. I didn't go to a fancy culinary school. As I saw it, I was just a guy from Garland who cooks barbecue for a living.

What I've come to believe is that the titles aren't all that important. You can call me chef or not, and it doesn't have an effect on the food I cook. What's important to me is my relationship with food, family, and my customers. Looking back as far as I can remember, most of my memories involve food and the people gathered around the table. I love to revisit the smell of a whole hog that just finished cooking at our annual family get-together. I'm still inspired by the crunchy deep-fried Spanish mackerel I first tasted as a teenager. There's my first Delta tamale on a road trip through Mississippi, my first taste of true Italian gravy at a table next to my girlfriend (now my wife) . . . heck, I can still remember the Bojangles' chicken biscuit I ate just a few hours before my daughter, Taylor Grace, was born.

Okay, so I'm a food-loving chef. But the way I see it, that's not at the top of the list. First and foremost, I am a barbecue guy. While most people now know me for Southern Smoke, the barbecue restaurant in Garland, North Carolina, my own barbecue journey started not in a restaurant but with a book: *Holy Smoke: The Big Book of North Carolina Barbecue*. In that book, John Shelton Reed, along with his wife, Dale, and William McKinney dove deep into the cultural significance and history of barbecue in my state. It inspired me to start my own barbecue journey, using traditional techniques that had fallen by the wayside. (Now that I know him, I often joke with John that if he hadn't written that book, I might not be in the barbecue business!)

I was soon obsessed, smoking in my backyard every chance I got—not with the intention of opening a restaurant, but to preserve a small part of my history as a North Carolinian and to pass a skill down to my children. I sat up night after night in the rain, heat, and cold learning and trying to get better with each cook. As I began to get better at my craft, I started offering free barbecue to anyone who would take it. As the word began to spread, my phone began to ring from people wanting me to cook barbecue for them. Slowly but surely, I began to realize that maybe I could make a living doing something that I loved. While barbecue wasn't in my blood, it slowly became a part of my soul.

When I first started working on this book, I sat down with three important Southern men and asked the question: "Why is cooking barbecue so important to us?" What ensued was a wide-ranging discussion not just about cooking

barbecue, but about the cultural significance in our communities. We talked about the hog-killing days, as they called it, where communities would begin early in the day and work until late at night preparing every usable part of the pig. We talked about how that was a real event and how barbecue as a hobby is still very much something to do with friends and family.

As I went back through that conversation, I realized much of Southern food shares this DNA with the stories told around the table about barbecue. I've seen this at our restaurant as well: Unique Southern sides bring up memories and strike a nerve with certain customers. In this book, I'll revisit many of those dishes, such as James Island Shrimp Pie (page 96), Merigold Tomatoes (page 151), and Chocolate Chess Pie

with Pecans (page 181). You'll notice that I do take some liberties with them, though this is done with love. Mostly what I try to do is incorporate some of today's values, like using fresh, local ingredients whenever possible. (Though sometimes I do use a chef-type technique, like that used in the Brown Butter Creamed Corn recipe on page 73.)

One last thing you'll find in this book is a few trips down side roads—places where I wanted to share the history of a dish or ingredient. Until I started cooking for a living, I admit I didn't understand where the dishes I grew up eating came from and why it was important to understand their history. Through this book, I hope you will have a better understanding of why these parts of the South cook the way we do and why it's so important to us to keep these dishes and recipes alive.

BARBECUE BASICS

So you want to cook barbecue? While you can cook barbecue on a grill, barbecuing is not the same as firing up the grill to cook hot dogs and hamburgers. Cooking barbecue is something that takes time; it's all about low temperature and a slow pace to develop those sought-after smoky flavors.

As you learn the basics of barbecuing, not everything will turn out perfectly. Because large cuts of meat take a long time to smoke properly, my advice is to start out small. Smoke some wings (page 86) or chicken quarters (page 47). Then try some ribs (page 124). Only once you get the feel for your grill should you try larger cuts of meat, such as pork butt (page 42).

What you choose to smoke with is a personal choice. You can smoke with a regular backyard grill, a pellet smoker, or even a huge reverse-airflow smoker—the kind you see at competitions. While there's a reason the big, expensive smokers are popular for the obsessed, you don't need one to smoke meat at home. In fact, I started out in my backyard, smoking on a little charcoal grill you could find at any chain hardware store. I smoked anything I could get my hands on month after month and eventually jumped to a 12-foot (3.5 m) reverse-airflow monster. (I named her Jezebel.) That's a big jump, but I knew I was obsessed!

I'm not here to sell you on what type of grill or smoker is best. Everyone's needs are different. Instead, in this chapter I will do my best to explain what I've learned over the years in the hope it will help you on your own barbecue journey.

FIRE, FUEL, AND FRIENDS

You don't need a ton of equipment to get started in barbecue, but you will need to make a few important decisions as you get going. First, you'll need a grill or smoker, the source of your fire. Then you'll need to figure out your fuel—a.k.a. choosing your wood. Last but not least, you have got to find yourself a few good friends willing to embark on the barbecue journey with you. Once you get into smoking large cuts of meat, which can take at least eight hours or more, you'll be glad to have company.

FIRE

The first thing you'll need, and the most expensive, is a grill or smoker to harness your fire. As I've already mentioned, there is nothing wrong with starting small. Here are some advantages and disadvantages of the main choices, as well as what to look for:

- **The basic setup:** For a starter setup you can't go wrong with a Weber Kettle grill. It's a great all-around tool that you can use to grill burgers or smoke a whole Boston butt. They can be found at most large hardware store chains.

- **The middle road:** Once you get into smoking and you want to elevate your barbecue game, a pellet smoker, such as a Traeger grill, is a nice next step. Cooking with a pellet smoker means you don't have to worry about finding and curing wood (discussed on page 17). They also eliminate the strain of constantly adding wood to an existing fire as most models have a hopper to constantly feed your smoker with pellets.

- **The high end:** When you talk about true stick burner pits, you don't need to look any further than Lang brand smokers. They offer several different models, from the 36-inch (91 cm) series, which is perfect for your backyard patio, to the 108-inch (274 cm) series, which can be found behind some of the South's finest barbecue restaurants.

When trying to decide on a smoker, you need to take several factors into account. The first thing is budget. It can be tough to pull together a few thousand dollars for a high-end smoker—and to be honest, I wouldn't recommend it if you're just starting out. Make sure you love cooking barbecue—like you-want-to-cook-for-competitions love it—before you drop that kind of money. Start out small and work your way up!

Ask yourself how much you're going to use the grill or smoker. Think about what you're going to be cooking and whom you are going to be cooking for. If you are just going to be cooking for your family, you shouldn't need a huge cooking surface. If you plan on throwing a party or hosting a tailgate every weekend, you will need a big cooking surface (and possibly a pull-behind smoker on a trailer!).

The most important thing to keep in mind is quality. Whatever grill you buy needs to be well-built. Move the smoker around, open the lid, and check the metal to see how thick it is. As a rule of thumb, if it feels well-built and is heavy, it will be a good smoker. On the other hand, thin metal won't hold heat very well, which means you will constantly be adding wood to your fire to keep

the temperature in the correct range. Likewise, if the lid isn't heavy and well-built, smoke will pour out of the seams. Finally, it's worth checking the dampers to see if they will slide easily. As metal heats, it expands, which will only make sticky dampers harder to adjust.

FUEL

Okay, you've got your grill or smoker sorted out. The next thing you need to decide is what type of fuel you want to use. I recommend using lump charcoal to start any fire, whether it's for a longer 10-hour cook or just grilling out a pork loin. Charcoal is just to get the fire started, though. To smoke meat, you'll rely on wood.

No matter what type of wood you choose, make sure you're buying cured wood. Smoking with green wood (fresh wood that has just been cut) is notoriously hard due to the amount of moisture in it. On the other hand, you don't want to use wood that is too dry. Anything that has been kiln dried, such as the bags of wood you often find at the hardware store, is great wood for grilling a steak or pork chops. However, you'll want to stay away from this type of wood when you're smoking. In fact, most bagged woods are kiln dried, which means they will burn too quickly. (You can soak them, but it's extremely difficult to get just the right amount of moisture in them without waterlogging them and putting out your fire.) Cured wood is the way to go.

A QUICK LOOK AT WOOD

Some woods will dramatically change the flavor profile of your meat, so I recommend starting out with a light-flavored wood, such as oak, and then building your way up to something like mesquite. Because some folks love the taste of heavy smoke and others just want a hint, there's no magic formula that will work for everyone. Here are my 2 cents on the most common woods.

OAK	Known for its mellow flavor, oak is a perfect wood for smoking most meats—and it's beginner friendly. I find the flavor is ideal for beef, chicken, ribs, turkey, and any cut of pork.
HICKORY	Hickory is another versatile wood. It lends an almost sweet flavor through its smoke, though you do have to be careful. If you cook too long with heavy hickory smoke, your meat can take on a bitter flavor. Try hickory with beef, turkey, and pork.
MESQUITE	Mesquite wood packs an intense flavor. You have to be very careful when using it, as you can go from a touch of smoke to over-the-top smoky quickly. I recommend getting a few hours on the smoker under your belt before you use mesquite. It's especially nice for smoking beef.
PECAN	I find pecan has a rich, sweet, and almost nutty flavor. Many people mix it with another hard wood to tone down the distinctive flavor. Try it for ribs, chicken, and turkey.
APPLE	Apple wood is mild and sweet. However, it takes a while for apple wood to permeate the meat, so use it only on sections of meat you'll be smoking for a long time if you want to develop that rich, sweet flavor. It's perfect for ribs and chicken.

When it comes to wood size, you'll have a few options. The purest form of cooking barbecue would, of course, start with split pieces of wood. This can be a bit problematic if you are cooking on a small backyard grill that won't hold an 18-inch (46 cm) piece of wood. If you have access to a table saw, you can cut the wood into smaller pieces that will fit in your grill. Another option is wood pellets, which are made from compacted sawdust and come in a wide variety of flavors. They make it easy to work with different flavor profiles. They also tend to burn both hotter and more slowly than whole pieces of wood.

As for the type of wood, at my restaurant we mostly use white oak, with a mix of some red oak depending on what's available. Oak is a wood that is pretty easy to come by, and I also like the mellow smoke flavor it gives meat. However, depending on where you live and what is available, you'll need to play around with different woods. In most parts of the country you can find common woods such as hickory, cherry, and apple that have been cured and are ready to go.

Note: The best place to find wood is often right in your own backyard or the yard of a friend or neighbor. Almost everyone loves a hand with brush cleanup, and you may walk away with some nice pieces of oak! Just make sure you aren't stuck chopping pine or another wood not suitable for smoking. Once you've got your wood, find a nice dry place or a shed and let it dry out. In about a month you will have cured wood that is ready to cook with.

FRIENDS

A lot of people overlook this last essential ingredient, but it's one of the things that make barbecue a special hobby: You absolutely need to find a few good friends to barbecue with you! Now what you're looking for here is a couple of folks as crazy as you, willing to stay up all night smoking meat. (Ideally, they'll be great storytellers as well.) While you might think you can go it alone, take it from someone who has sat up a lot of nights cooking by myself—it's just not as fun. At best, it might be enjoyable for a few hours . . . but at some point toward dawn, you'll end up talking to yourself. Over the years, my barbecue buddies have become some of my best friends. The stories we have shared created a bond that can only be formed around a fire, cooking all night.

OTHER USEFUL ITEMS

After you have the big three covered, the first item I recommend buying is a notebook. As I started getting serious about smoking, I started taking notes. I would record things like how long I cooked the meat, what type(s) of wood I used, if there were any issues, even what the weather was like (yes, I have barbecued in a snowstorm . . . at the beach none the less). Then, most importantly, what was the result? Tasting notes are every bit as crucial as cooking notes.

Another item I recommend is a digital instant-read thermometer. Accurate temperatures are crucial when cooking barbecue. Even after years of practice, when I think I could barbecue in my sleep, I still use one every day. Especially when you start out, though, without a reliable thermometer, how will you know if your chicken is done or way past done, or if the Boston butt stalled?

You'll find a good pair of heavy-duty gloves are useful from start to finish. From the very beginning as you get the charcoal started, you'll be generating a good amount of heat, so don't wait to put on your gloves. And opt for longer gloves that cover your forearms. Trust me: When you pull that first Boston butt off the grill and pig grease runs down your forearm, you will regret not buying the longer gloves (though I say it's okay to proudly display minor barbecue burns at work on Monday if you'd like). Also, if you do get burned, try covering the burn in yellow mustard. Seriously! It works.

A small pan for water will prove useful when smoking (see page 22). You can use a disposable foil pan or a small restaurant pan, if you have room. If you don't have much room, a metal coffee can will work!

HOW TO SET UP A GRILL FOR SMOKING

There are a few things you'll need to juggle on just about any grill: your fuel source (coal and wood), your meat, and a water pan. Let's run through them in that order.

Most grills have a way for you to put your fuel source on one side and periodically add extra fuel to your existing fire. On some grills, this can be done by leaving a grate out on one side of the grill. Alternatively, on other grills, such as kettle-style grills, you can flip part of the grate open to add more fuel. When smoking, you want your fuel source to be as far away from your meat as possible. You should also try to place the meat on the area of the grill where the smoke will be exiting. In short, you want to make sure you get as much of the flow of smoke over the surface of the meat as you possibly can. (Another advantage to having your fuel source at the opposite end from the meat is that it will allow you to add more wood and charcoal throughout the cooking process without moving the meat.)

If this is sounding abstract, think of the opposite scenario, which you don't want: If you place a whole Boston butt over a live flame, not only will it cook too fast, but once the grease gets flowing, it will drip right on the fire, causing flare-ups. Burned is never the flavor profile you are going for!

When it comes to placing the meat, there are a few considerations. If you're smoking only one type of meat, this is the simplest setup because you need to consider only one type of food. Once you have a few smoking sessions under your belt, there's nothing wrong with smoking more than one type of meat at a time, or even mixing in some grilling with your smoking. The trick is to figure out about how long it takes to cook each thing and where you will need to place it at different times during the cook. Hot and fast things like burgers and flank steak will need to be cooked directly over the fire, whereas other items like ribs and Boston butts need to be cooked away from the fire. Careful planning is needed because you'll need to limit the amount of time your grill lid is open to minimize losing temperature in your grill.

Now that you've got your plan for where to place the fuel and the meat, you're almost done. However, there's one last thing you will need to plan for before you're ready to dump your coals and start smoking: a water pan. The water pan serves two purposes. The main reason to use a water pan is to help with humidity. During the cooking process, the air in your smoker will naturally become dry. Evaporation from the water pan will create humidity, which will keep the meat from drying out during a long smoke. Second, placing a small water pan under what you are cooking will help with cleanup after you cook because it will catch excess grease or seasoning that may fall off during the cooking process.

Note: Some people get creative with the water pan. For example, I've tried adding apple juice to the pan when cooking ribs. When the sweet apple juice evaporates, you will get an added layer of sugar on your ribs.

LET'S GET SMOKING

Now that we have the grill setup planned, let's go ahead and get a fire going. Don't get me wrong, building a fire from twigs is fun—but it's also very time-consuming. Using charcoal and a chimney starter is quicker, foolproof, and reliable. Here's how to do it:

1. Crumple up newspaper or junk mail and stuff it underneath the chimney. Make sure you don't overfill it; if you do, you will not get any air into your fire and it won't burn properly.

2. Fill the charcoal to the top of the chimney. There's no need to fill the chimney to the point where it is overflowing; you will add wood during the cooking process. The charcoal is just to get the fire going.

3. Light the newspaper in the bottom of the chimney, making sure you have adequate airflow to the charcoal. As the flames begin to overtake the charcoal, you will begin to hear some pops and see sparks.

4. Let the charcoal burn down until it is mostly bright red. The flame at the top of the chimney will sometimes resemble a jet engine.

At this point your chimney is ready, but it's going to be very hot. Using heavy-duty gloves, slowly pour the charcoal into the correct spot on your grill. From here, you'll need an understanding of the elements of a good fire and how to control it. It's time to add some wood. Start with your smallest piece or two, ensuring that you don't overcrowd your fire. What you want is a good fire that slowly builds. Once your first pieces of wood begin to burn, start adding more pieces until you have a large enough fire for your grill (see the photo on page 27 for a sense of fire size). When you have a good fire established, close the lid or door.

As you add the wood, there are other considerations to keep in mind. No matter how long your wood has cured or dried, there will still be a bit of moisture in it. How much moisture is in the wood will affect the amount of time it takes to get the wood up to a consistent fire that's burning well. Higher moisture in the wood will also cool down your fire because it will take a longer amount of time to cook the moisture out of the wood. Don't get frustrated with a "bad" fire or a slow-starting fire. You'll find all fires are different. Sometimes you'll get one that will burn perfectly, then the next one will be all over the place—even when the wood is from the same pile.

Besides wood moisture, the other main variable is the air. To get a good, consistent fire going, you have to find the perfect balance of air. You want to encourage the fire to grow, but you don't want it roaring in no time. The amount of airflow in your grill is controlled with dampers, either on the side or on the top.

Keep in mind that all grills and smokers are different. Some have great insulation, while some have poor insulation; some have an offset firebox, while others don't. You will have to learn your own personal sweet spot through your first few sessions. Once you find it, you won't forget it! I can tell you that on my smoker, Jezebel, the smoke stack damper needs to be 80 percent open, the left side firebox vent needs to be 50 percent open, the back needs to be closed, and the right side vent needs to be barely open. Just like my anniversary, it's engraved into my memory!

COOKING AND MAINTAINING THE FIRE

Now that your fire is going, it's almost time to get the meat in place (make sure to add the water pan as well if you haven't done so already). The fire you built should be good for about the first hour, but you shouldn't add the meat immediately. You'll have to wait for the right kind of smoke.

Learning how to read smoke is a skill, but it's a fun one to learn. Staring at smoke billowing from a fire that you made with your own hands is as primal as it gets, and most barbecue lovers find it magical. However, the smoke also provides valuable information. By watching your smoke carefully, you can get a sense of what's going on with your fire without opening the grill to check it.

Smoke will go through three distinct stages. The first stage is a heavy, thick smoke. Usually at the beginning of the cook, this smoke will be so thick it's hard to see through. I recommend waiting out this smoke and letting the fire calm down a bit before putting any meat on. Even if the meat is not directly over the fire, it will still be too hot, and you risk developing undesirable flavors. The second stage, when the smoke is not as thick, is what you're waiting for. The best way I can describe this smoke is to think of the way smoke rolls out of the chimney of a house. It's consistent, but not flowing fast. When your smoke is at this stage, your fire has the perfect balance of air. Now it's time to get the meat on the grill or smoker.

Once your meat is on the grill, you can let the fire burn until the smoke tells you it's starting to dwindle. During this last stage, as the fire dies down, the smoke will decrease, and if you leave for a few minutes and come back, you might not even see any smoke at all. Yet you can still feel the heat coming out of your grill. When this happens, it's time to add more wood to get the fire going again and producing smoke.

Note: Reading smoke is great, but you should also monitor a thermometer once you have meat smoking. It will tell you the internal temperature of the smoker, and you'll need to keep a close eye on that temperature to make sure you're not cooking your meat too fast or too slow. If your fire is too cool, you can let some additional air in; if it's too hot, you can restrict the airflow to starve it a bit. This adjustment is straightforward and easy to master in a smoking session or two.

You have to be careful when you are adding your wood to your fire. As many fires as I have managed, I am still very cautious. I also have a few scars to remind me of the times that I wasn't cautious enough. You have to understand that your fire has been ripping for at least an hour at the first addition, and sometimes hours between additions. Heavy-duty gloves are key. Never touch or grab any part of the grill or smoker with your bare hand.

If you are using a small grill such as a Weber, adding extra wood can get tricky. If you have small pieces of wood, you can slide the extra wood under the flip-up edge. However, if you are using larger pieces of wood, which I recommend because they will burn longer, you will have to remove the grate with the meat on it. It's easy with a friend, but it takes a little planning if you are by yourself. You will need a stable, heatproof surface to put the grate on. Ideally, you want to cover the surface with butcher paper or foil because grease will be coming off the meat. (Be careful when you are transferring the grate and meat, because the hot grease will drip. You don't want it on your feet and legs.) Once you have removed the grate, keep your gloves on and slowly add the wood to the top of the fire. Place your grill grate back on and continue smoking.

Keep in mind that every time you open your grill, you are losing heat, which means extra time getting your grill back up to temperature. When you are adding wood, do it as quickly as you can while maintaining safety standards. Even if you want to show your buddy who just walked up how pretty that rack of ribs is looking, just wait! Let them "oooh" and "ahhh" and post on social media when you're finished.

For all but the smallest cuts of meat, you will go through the process of adding wood several times. If your smoke isn't perfect all the time, don't panic; it will mellow back out. What you want to avoid is having heavy smoke during the entire cooking process because you will surely have overly smoky meats. (Some folks like a heavy smoke, but what I'm talking about is too smoky even for them—trust me.) With some practice, you will get to the point with timing that your fire will slowly die out as you finish your cooking, though of course that's not necessary. If your meat is done, remove it from the fire!

GUIDELINES FOR COMMON MEATS

In the list that follows, I'll provide some benchmark temperatures and times for smoking common meats. However, keep in mind that these are recommended temperatures and times only; don't drive yourself crazy trying to stay dialed in to exactly 250°F (120°C) for 4 hours. Cooking times are an average, as sometimes meat will cook very easy and quickly, and other times it will be stubborn and cook slowly. The key is hitting your internal temperature.

	COOKING TEMPERATURE	COOKING TIME	INTERNAL TEMPERATURE
CHICKEN WINGS	225°F to 235°F (107°C to 113°C)	2 hours	165°F (74°C) if not frying; 155°F (68°C) if deep-frying after smoking
CHICKEN QUARTERS	250°F to 260°F (121°C to 127°C)	3 hours	167°F (75°C)
WHOLE BEEF FILLET (without using the oven)	275°F to 300°F (135°C to 149°C)	55 minutes	Medium-rare: 125°F (52°C) Medium: 145°F (63°C) Medium-well: 150°F (66°C) Well-done: 160°F (71°C)
BABY BACK RIBS	240°F to 250°F (116°C to 121°C)	3½ to 4 hours	177°F (81°C)
BOSTON BUTT/WHOLE PORK SHOULDER	240°F to 250°F (116°C to 121°C)	1 hour per pound	195°F to 205°F (91°C to 96°C) degrees

WHAT ABOUT THE WEATHER?

As if there weren't enough variables, the weather will indeed affect your day or night of smoking—especially any type of moisture. Personally, I often deal with hot and humid summers. During these times, my biggest battle is getting a good, hot fire built quickly. When you're smoking, weather conditions such as rain and snow may come into play. If you get caught out in the elements, do your best to keep your wood from absorbing any excess moisture. I recommend buying a large tarp or storing your wood in a shed.

Don't look at the elements as the enemy, though. I actually cook my best barbecue on rainy, damp nights. The moisture in the air just helps in the cooking process. Customers in the know will always show up on days after it has rained all night long. They greet me with something like, "It rained last night, so I knew I should stop by!" Hmm . . . maybe I should put a sprinkler system on the roof and run it every night!

TIPS AND TRICKS

When you're smoking meat, you are going to run into problems. Here are a few tricks to help you deliver great barbecue even when you hit some of the common bumps in the road.

A common complaint when you start out smoking is dry chicken—especially white meat. The secret to moist chicken on a smoker is found in every grocery store in America: cheap squirt butter. (Yes, the same butter you have walked by a million times and never bought.) Squirt butter is mainly made up of vegetable oil—most brands keep it around 60 percent. As your chicken nears the point of finishing (the last hour or so), begin squirting butter over the top of the meat. The vegetable oil and butter will melt and keep your chicken moist and tender.

The biggest roadblock that you will hit usually comes when you tackle something like your first Boston butt: We call it "the stall." Typically only a problem with larger cuts, the stall is caused by moisture evaporating from the surface of the meat. It cools the meat just like the human body is cooled by sweat.

You have two options for getting the meat to the finish line. The first thing you can do, if you have time, is increase your heat a bit and let the piece of meat just push through the stall. This could add an hour or so to your cooking time, but it will push through and catch up; in fact, your heat will rise pretty quickly.

The other strategy for overcoming a stall is called the Texas Crutch. I've never been able to track down where the name came from, but it appears to have surfaced on the competition barbecue trail as a way to keep moisture in brisket. If you'd like to try the Texas Crutch, at the point of the stall, quickly wrap the entire piece of meat in foil. This keeps the humidity contained instead of letting it escape to cool down the grill or smoker. In my experience, this technique can work well. However, I recommend using it for only an hour or so. Once you get through the stall, you will likely want to unwrap your meat to let it finish cooking to ensure you develop a crunchy bark on the outside. If you leave it in the foil, even the outside will stay very soft.

My last tip—at least the last one I'm willing to share today—involves the Texas Crutch again, but this time with ribs. Normally your ribs aren't going to stall, but you can use this trick to produce beautifully sweet, fall-off-the-bone ribs. Once you have smoked your ribs for a few hours and they have reached a temperature of 145°F to 155°F (63°C to 68°C), pull them off the cooking surface. Lay the racks on foil lengthwise, ensuring the ribs are in the middle. Sprinkle the ribs with a handful of brown sugar, then wrap the ribs in the foil. Seal the foil at the top, making sure you don't wrap them too tightly—you don't want your bark to be pulled off. Cook for about an hour to steam your ribs and make them separate from the bone.

REMOVING MEAT FROM THE GRILL

It's time to enjoy the fruits of your labor. This is yet another time when you are going to need those heavy-duty gloves because, guess what, whatever you are cooking is very hot! Take your time and be careful while transferring the meat to a pan or cutting board; grease is going to splash around, and it is very hot. This is when you want to get your phone out to take lots of pictures, and make sure you have friends around so that they can be wowed by your barbecue skills!

THE BARK
AND THE
SMOKE RING

Many barbecue lovers are all about the bark. The bark is the dark mahogany-colored exterior that you often see on smoked meats. It is created when you add just the right amount of rub to the outside of your meat and then hit it with just the right amount of smoke over a long period of time. It is tricky creating a perfect bark; if you cook at too low of a heat, you won't get bark, and if you cook at too high of a temperature, you will have a char on the outside of your meat. But if you stay on top of your temperatures and times, you'll get that perfect bite of bark that barbecue lovers and aficionados search for.

For the uninitiated, the smoke ring is usually just below the surface of the bark and is a bright pink color. While many people believe it is a symbol of great barbecue, a deep, huge smoke ring doesn't automatically make meat amazing. It is part of a larger whole.

What causes the smoke ring, and how do you get one every time? Myoglobin is a protein that gives meat its red color. Beef has the most myoglobin in it, followed by pork, dark-meat chicken, and then white-meat chicken. Myoglobin loves to bind with oxygen. When you begin to burn wood, it creates carbon dioxide. As the gas dissolves on the wet meat, the oxygen atoms bind with the myoglobin and form that prized smoke ring. This means if you want to get a deep, well-defined smoke ring, the trick is keeping your meat surface wet. A piece of meat with a dry surface simply won't accept smoke as well. I recommend using a mop or a squirt bottle to keep your meat as moist as possible. Note that once your meat hits the 160°F to 170°F (71°F to 77°F) range, you will not get much more smoke penetration.

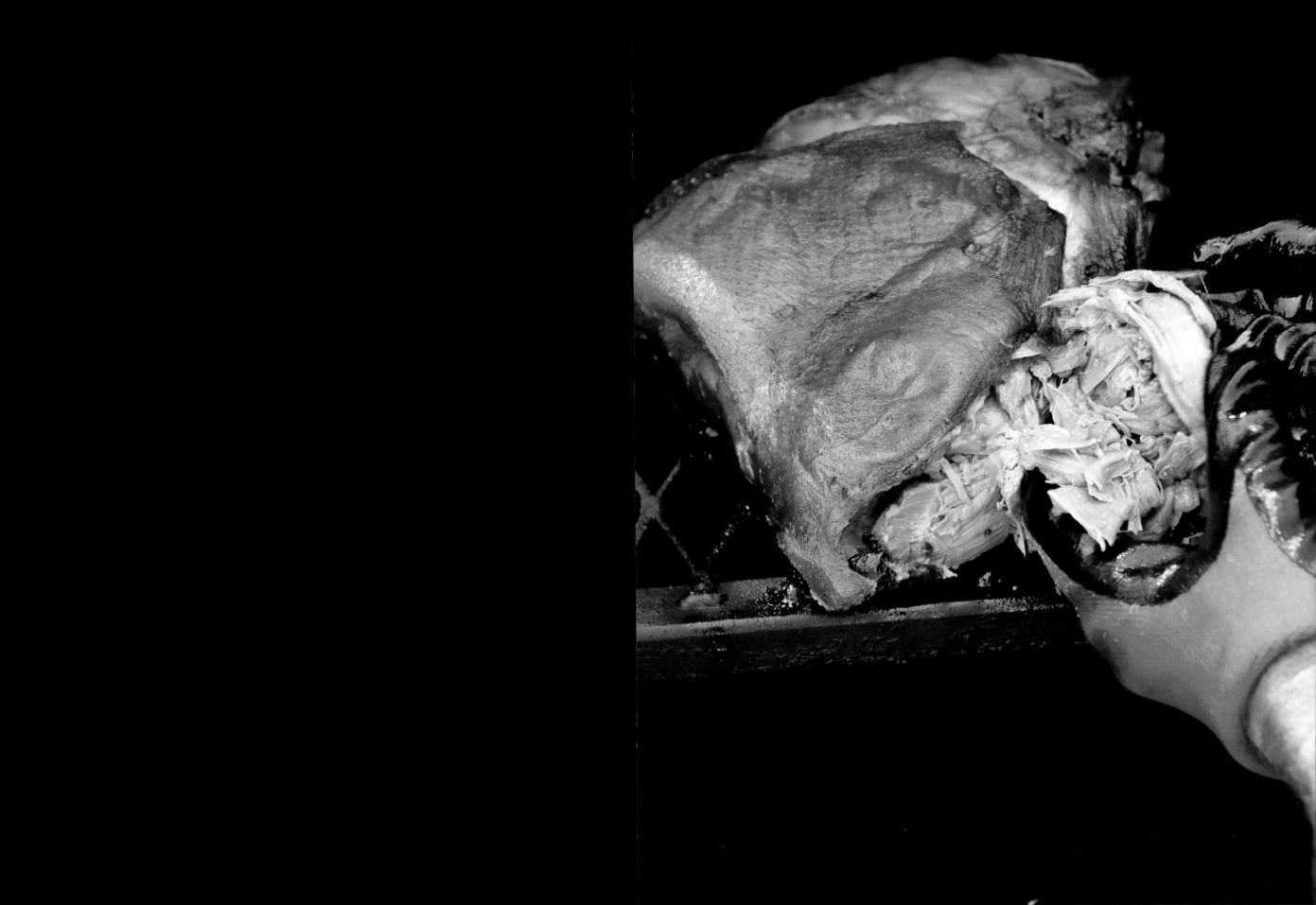

MY RULES FOR GOOD BARBECUE

I have a few strong thoughts about barbecue I want to share before sending you on your way to explore the rest of the book. Feel free to argue with your friends about which school of barbecue is best, but in my opinion the following facts are nonnegotiable:

Great barbecue takes time. When I say this, I mean both that a smoking session takes hours and that learning how to master your own grill or smoker will take an investment of time. That said, if you put in the time, you will (eventually) make great barbecue.

Barbecue should be shared. Sure, sharing the meat you smoke is the name of the game, but why not share the process as well? A unique comradery forms around a fire.

Related to that last point, barbecue should be shared with kids. Don't think of a hobby that involves fire as something for adults only. Be safe, but let kids be involved to some degree. If they ask questions, try your best to answer them! We live in a microwave world where we want things quick, fast, and easy. Barbecue can show kids the value in slowing down and taking your time to do something the proper way—not just the fast way. It's a hobby that can provide a lifetime of memories (and full bellies).

Give yourself enough time. Always build in extra time for the unexpected. If you are having a dinner party, try to have your meat done an hour before the guests are supposed to arrive. There is not much worse than having 30 friends staring at you waiting to eat dinner!

Have fun. Barbecue should be something you look forward to! After all these years, I still get excited to build my next fire. I love the challenge of cooking over long periods of time. I even love solving the occasional problems and hiccups that crop up. Hopefully, you will too.

NORTH CAROLINA

Pork, Vinegar, and Collards

"Are you a fan of eastern-style or western-style barbecue?" That seemingly harmless question has started heated conversations between North Carolinians since barbecue was thrust to the forefront of our culinary culture centuries ago. What can I say? We take great pride in our barbecue, and we have since colonial times. One of the first documented pig pickin' events in our state's history took place in Wilmington, North Carolina, a full seven years before the Boston Tea Party. (Of course, it was to feed a large group of local militia who opposed the Stamp Act.) Barbecue has been our thing ever since.

That said, the division between who has the best, east or west, makes me cringe. I know people will soon get angry at one another and feelings will be hurt. Because I grew up in eastern North Carolina, there was a time in my life when I would never have uttered the words that I liked western-style barbecue, but through my life and my travels I have learned an important lesson: Good barbecue is good barbecue no matter what dirt is under your feet.

In this chapter, I'll explore some of the dishes and traditions from both sides of the state, though with an admitted bias to the east, where I grew up and where I still live and cook to this day. You will have to make up your own mind which you prefer. All I can say is that I encourage you to try it all—take a road trip if you can!

SMOKED BOSTON BUTT WITH EASTERN NORTH CAROLINA VINEGAR SAUCE

Serves 6 to 8

| 1 whole Boston butt, about 8–10 pounds (3.5 to 4.5 kg) | 1½ cups (355 ml) Eastern North Carolina Vinegar Sauce (page 44) | ¼ cup (14.5 g) red pepper flakes |

When it comes to the difference between eastern and western North Carolina barbecue, it's not all about the sauce. The differences begin with the pig itself. In the eastern part of the state, the traditional method is to fire whole hogs over oak coals. Then the chef pulls and chops the meat, finishing it with red pepper flakes and salty, spicy vinegar sauce. In the western part of the state, the tradition has been to cook pork shoulders over hickory coals. The meat is coarsely chopped and served with a tomato-based sauce affectionately known as dip. (If you like the tougher meat from the outside of the shoulder, you can try asking for a little "outside brown.")

I admit I prefer the eastern style, but then again that's where I'm from! I love the taste of the vinegar sauce cutting through the fatty pork—and of course the hit of heat from the red pepper flakes. But don't get me wrong. I can find myself craving a little piece of outside brown dipped in that sweet sauce from the west.

For the recipe that follows, you'll smoke a pork shoulder as I believe that's the best way to smoke pork at home. Teaching how to pit barbecue would eat up more pages than it's worth in a book not devoted to the topic. And the reality is, if you use oak wood and vinegar sauce to dress the meat, you can get pretty darn close to traditional eastern barbecue with this recipe—no cinder blocks required! If you're interested in trying out the western style, see page 45 for the sauce recipe and modifications to the cooking process.

Prepare a smoker according to the instructions on page 25, using oak if you can. Place the Boston butt on the prepared smoker fat cap side up. This way the fat will cook through and drip down the meat the entire time it is on the grill, keeping the meat tender. Cook for 8 to 10 hours, or until the butt reaches an internal temperature of 195°F (91°C). See page 31 for tips on working through "the stall," a common challenge when smoking Boston butt and other large cuts of meat.

When the butt is finished, carefully pull the meat off the bone. You will want to let the meat cool for a few minutes first; I recommend pulling the middle part of the butt open and letting the steam pour out. When you pull the meat, discard any solid fat and gristle.

Once the meat has been pulled and cleaned, place it on a cutting board and lightly chop it with a cleaver. Transfer the chopped meat to a bowl. Toss it with the Eastern North Carolina Vinegar Sauce and red pepper flakes, starting with about 1 cup (235 ml) of the sauce and adding more to taste. Serve hot.

(sauce recipe follows)

EASTERN NORTH CAROLINA VINEGAR SAUCE

Makes 1 gallon (3.8 l)

1 gallon (3.8 l) apple cider vinegar

1¼ cups (360 g) salt

2 tablespoons cayenne pepper

3½ tablespoons (25 g) paprika

1 tablespoon red pepper flakes

This is my recipe for a classic eastern-style sauce. Make sure you shake it well before using it because most of the spices will settle to the bottom as it sits. When you are saucing your barbecue, remember to lightly sauce it and let people add extra if they want it. You can add more, but you can't take it out. If I bite into a barbecue sandwich and the first thing I taste is sauce, I immediately think the pit master is trying to hide something from me. Each bite should be a balance of smoke, pork, and sauce. So add a little sauce and taste it, then adjust from there.

In a large stockpot, bring the vinegar and salt to a boil over high heat. When the mixture begins to boil, add the cayenne, paprika, and red pepper flakes. Stir the mixture with a ladle until combined and remove from the heat. The finished cooled sauce can be stored in the empty vinegar gallon jug. It can be stored in a dry, dark place for a month or refrigerated for slightly longer. Shake well before using!

WESTERN NORTH CAROLINA-STYLE
BARBECUE

If you want to try western North Carolina–style barbecue, here's what you should do. First, switch out the wood in your smoker to hickory if you can find some locally. Whip up a batch of Western North Carolina BBQ Sauce (see below) while the pork starts to cook. Then during the last three hours of smoking, mop or baste the meat with the sauce periodically.

Once you take the meat off the heat and let it cool enough to handle, don't pull and toss it with the eastern sauce. Instead, remove any gristle or large chunks of fat and chop the meat into small chunks. Serve with additional western sauce on the side to use as a dip.

WESTERN NORTH CAROLINA BBQ SAUCE

Makes 3 cups (750 g)

2 cups (475 ml) apple cider vinegar

¾ cup (180 g) ketchup

2 tablespoons (30 ml) hot sauce

½ cup (115 g) packed brown sugar

3 tablespoons (54 g) salt

2 tablespoons red pepper flakes

2 teaspoons freshly ground black pepper

Traditionally, this sauce is served on the side as a dip, though it can be used to baste meat as well. I've found plenty of uses for it beyond pork, like chicken cooked on the grill.

In a medium pot over medium-low heat, whisk all ingredients together until well combined. Cook for 15 minutes, stirring occasionally. Store in an airtight container in the refrigerator until ready to use. It will keep for a few months in the refrigerator.

SMOKED CHICKEN QUARTERS WITH PAPA NIPPER'S CHURCH SAUCE

Serves 6

6 chicken quarters (leg and thigh
section still connected)

3 tablespoons (54 g) salt

1½ tablespoons freshly ground
black pepper

½ cup (1 stick, 112 g) butter

1 cup (225 g) packed brown sugar

2 tablespoons garlic salt

3 cups (710 ml) Eastern North Carolina
Vinegar Sauce (page 44)

My wife's grandfather, Jimmy Nipper, comes from a barbecue family. His father owned Dan's Old Fashion BBQ in Sanford, North Carolina, through the 1950s and 1960s. Jimmy spent much of his youth shoveling hardwood coals into pits night after night, cooking whole hogs. While his own career took him on a different path—into the North Carolina Highway Patrol—barbecue was always in his blood. He continued to cook for fund-raisers and church functions and became one of the most influential cooks in my own barbecue journey.

This recipe is my homage to the unique way he cooked chicken for church fund-raisers. Jimmy would cook whole chicken quarters over hardwood coals 'til they were almost done. Then, when the chickens were just short of finished, he would take them off the smoker and throw them in big coolers. He poured a vinegar-based sauce over them, closed the lid, and let them finish cooking in the cooler. While it sounds strange, what came out of the coolers was a smoky, juicy, vinegary, and somewhat sweet chicken that people couldn't get enough of.

Prepare a grill for smoking according to the instructions on page 25. Trim each chicken quarter of excess fat and skin, then season them liberally with salt and pepper. Arrange the quarters on the smoker and smoke for 2 hours at 250°F (120°C), or until a digital instant-read thermometer reads 165°F (75°C) when inserted deep into the meat.

While the chicken is smoking, melt the butter in a medium pot over medium heat. Add the brown sugar and whisk to combine. Add the garlic salt and vinegar sauce, reduce the heat to medium-low, and simmer for 15 minutes, stirring occasionally. Set the sauce aside and let it cool for 30 minutes.

(continued)

To finish the chicken, there are two options. The first way—the traditional way—requires a clean cooler. (A smallish cooler will work just fine here. If the cooler is too large, the chicken won't be immersed in the sauce.) Place the smoked chicken in the cooler and pour the sauce over the top. Close the lid and let the chicken rest for 30 minutes, or until you are ready to serve. Serve hot, straight from the cooler.

The other method—which works just fine but isn't quite as fun—is to use the oven. Preheat the oven to 200°F (95°C). Place the chicken in a casserole dish or a disposable foil pan and pour the sauce over the top. Cover the pan with foil and bake for 15 minutes. Serve hot.

BUTTERMILK FRIED CHICKEN *(pictured on page 51)*

Serves 4

1 whole chicken, butchered into 8 pieces (breasts, thighs, drumsticks, and wings)

1¼ teaspoons salt

1 teaspoon freshly ground black pepper

1 teaspoon paprika

1 quart (946 ml) buttermilk

3 cups (375 g) flour

Peanut or vegetable oil, for frying

Since the Middle Ages, the Scottish have fried chickens in fat, unlike most Europeans, who tend to broil or stew chicken. Naturally, as Scottish immigrants came to the southern United States, they brought their techniques for cooking chicken with them. These techniques slowly made their way across the South. Yet the true geniuses of fried chicken, the ones who helped shape it as an American staple, were the black women from West Africa—many of whom were working in the kitchens on plantations as slaves. They adopted the cooking methods of the Scots but added the flavors and spices that could be found only in West African cooking.

As the popularity of fried chicken grew, the increased demand for it resulted in some of the first black women entrepreneurs. These slaves would sell their fried chicken, biscuits, and pies to hungry travelers at train stations. Passing their goods through the passenger windows to hungry travelers, they created an extra income for their families.

Every time we eat a great piece of fried chicken, we should certainly look back and thank those who perfected this dish that we all have grown to adore. I like to brine my chicken in buttermilk for several reasons. Brining chicken makes it more tender. Also, the buttermilk helps add to the flavor of the chicken as it fries. I also like the fact that the buttermilk on the chicken helps the batter stick to the chicken, creating a uniform, crunchy crust.

(continued)

In a large bowl, season the chicken pieces with the salt, pepper, and paprika. Pour the buttermilk over the top of the chicken and make sure each piece is submerged. Refrigerate for a minimum of 30 minutes or up to 8 hours.

Remove the chicken from the refrigerator. Place the flour in a bowl. Pull the chicken pieces out of the buttermilk and let them drain on a wire rack or butcher paper. One by one, add each piece to the flour and toss, making sure it is evenly coated. For extra-crispy chicken, you can dip the coated chicken back into the buttermilk and then dip it back in the flour a second time.

In a Dutch oven, add oil until it is about 2½ inches (6 cm) deep. Heat the oil over medium heat to a temperature of 350°F (180°C). Flour should sizzle when it is sprinkled in the oil. Fry each piece of chicken for 12 to 15 minutes, or until it reaches an internal temperature of 167°F (74°C). Flip each piece in the middle of the frying to ensure it is golden brown on both sides.

You can fry more than one piece at a time, but don't crowd the Dutch oven or cook so much at once that the temperature drops far below 350°F (180°C). When the chicken has finished cooking, remove it from the grease and set on a clean wire rack to cool.

Buttermilk Fried Chicken (page 49) ▶

SMOKED TURKEY

Serves 8 to 10

For the Turkey

½ cup (120 ml) cooking oil
  (such as vegetable oil)

1 whole turkey (12 to 14 pounds
  [5.5 to 6.5 kg]), fully thawed

1 tablespoon garlic powder

2 teaspoons seasoned salt

2 teaspoons paprika

1 teaspoon salt

½ teaspoon freshly ground black pepper

½ teaspoon dried basil

1 cup (225 g) packed brown sugar

Mustard Cream Sauce with Thyme
  (page 54), optional, for serving

For the Stuffing

2 onions, halved and sliced

3 Granny Smith apples, cut into wedges

1 cup (225 g) packed brown sugar

Every Thanksgiving the same oven-roasted turkey is placed on the table year after year. Don't get me wrong, I love that oven-roasted bird—especially the huge turkey sandwiches smothered with Duke's Mayo that follow the night after Thanksgiving for lunch. I know there are other ways to do a turkey, such as deep-frying it, but that too seems a bit boring (well, it could get interesting if you don't pay attention while cooking!). Smoking a turkey will bring a whole new flavor of bird to your Thanksgiving meal. It is important to keep your bird moist throughout the cooking process. I recommend using squirt butter or a spray bottle with water. Try using it every 35 to 40 minutes, and remember to do this quickly to keep as much heat in your grill as possible. If your turkey looks a little dry, don't be scared to do this more often. We also add Granny Smith apples and brown sugar as a stuffing to add another element of flavor inside the bird.

To make the turkey: Prepare a smoker according to the directions on page 25, making sure it's running at a constant 250°F (120°C).

Pour the cooking oil over the turkey and use your hands to rub the oil all over the surface of the turkey until it is completely coated. In a small bowl, mix together the garlic powder, seasoned salt, paprika, salt, pepper, basil, and brown sugar until well combined. Set aside.

To make the stuffing: In a medium bowl, combine the onions, apples, and brown sugar with your hands.

Stuff the turkey with the apple mixture. Sprinkle the rub liberally on the turkey, rubbing it in with your hands to ensure the entire bird is covered. Gently place the turkey on the smoker breast side up, with the breast facing away from the direct heat. Smoke the turkey for 30 minutes per pound,

or until the breast meat registers 160°F (71°C). Remove the turkey from the smoker and place it on a baking sheet. Lightly tent the top with foil and let it rest for 30 minutes before slicing.

(sauce recipe follows)

MUSTARD CREAM SAUCE WITH THYME

Makes 1¹/₂ cups (355 ml)

4 tablespoons (55 g) butter

3 cloves garlic, minced

2 tablespoons (30 ml) white wine

¼ cup (44 g) yellow mustard

1 teaspoon salt

1 cup (235 ml) heavy cream

2 tablespoons chopped fresh thyme

In a saucepan over medium heat, melt the butter. Add the garlic and white wine and cook for 30 seconds, or until it becomes aromatic. Add the mustard, salt, and heavy cream. Whisk together until well combined. Add the thyme and cook for 6 to 8 minutes, whisking constantly to thicken the sauce and to prevent burning. When the sauce has thickened, remove it from the heat and serve with turkey or beef.

DON'T SKIP
THE DUKE'S

For the Tarter Sauce in this recipe (opposite), you'll notice that I call for Duke's Mayonnaise. Chances are that you're familiar with Duke's if you live in the South. However, in other parts of the country, Duke's isn't as popular as the "big" brands like Hellmann's and Kraft. That's a shame.

By all accounts, Duke's has been a hit in the South since Eugenia Duke first started selling the mayo commercially in 1923. Based in Greenville, South Carolina, Eugenia got her start making sandwiches and selling them to soldiers during World War I. With hungry men and women clamoring for her egg salad and ham salad, she soon figured out the secret was in her homemade mayonnaise. Once she started bottling that, the sandwiches were a thing of the past.

These days, Duke's is popular in the South, and also with professional chefs nationwide. Even chefs who are fanatical about making everything from scratch in their restaurants will often swear by store-bought for a couple of ingredients with signature flavors, like their favorite brand of ketchup or Duke's.

The debate rages on about why, exactly, Duke's stands head and shoulders above the rest. Those new to a jar of Duke's will quickly notice one difference: It's not as sweet as the competition. While brands like Miracle Whip trade on their sweetness, Duke's has no added sugar. This gives it greater flexibility in recipes, whether it's a recipe that wouldn't benefit from the added sweetness or a dish that already has other sweet ingredients (like potato salad with sweet relish).

So join the legions of chefs and Southerners who swear by Duke's. If you haven't already bought a jar, then give Duke's a try!

SALTINE CRACKER FRIED OYSTERS

Serves 4

For the Tartar Sauce

1½ cups (340 g) Duke's Mayonnaise
   (page 54)

½ medium red onion, finely diced

1 teaspoon freshly ground black pepper

2 tablespoons (30 ml) lemon juice

For the Oysters

2 dozen raw oysters, shucked

4 eggs

2 sleeves saltine crackers, crushed fine
   (about 3 cups, 215 g)

Vegetable oil, for frying

Sea salt

Lemon wedges

Oysters have long been a favorite in my family and for many others in my part of North Carolina. This recipe can be traced back to the kitchen of my great-grandmother, Grace Jarmen Hart. She would often fry up oysters in her home in Lenoir County to the delight of her husband, eight children, and pretty much anyone else in the neighborhood who dropped by that night. What set her oysters apart were the crushed-up saltine crackers used instead of flour and cornmeal to coat the outside of the oysters before frying. Turns out, this makes for a super-crunchy oyster. The tartar sauce you'll find here is also a family recipe, though from my grandmother, Dorothy Hart. Yes, it has a lot of onions in it . . . and no, you can't cut back on the onions!

To make the tartar sauce: In a small bowl, stir all of the ingredients until well combined. Refrigerate until ready to use.

To make the oysters: Drain the oysters in a colander and set aside. In a small mixing bowl, beat the eggs until they are a uniform consistency. Pour the crackers into a separate mixing bowl. Working in batches, add the oysters to the beaten eggs and roll them with a fork until they are completely coated. Transfer the oysters to the saltine mixture with a fork. Toss the oysters until they are completely covered with the cracker crumbs and set aside in a casserole dish. When all the oysters have been coated, place them in the refrigerator until you are ready to fry them.

In a heavy skillet, add oil until it is ½ inch (1 cm) deep. Heat the oil over medium heat until it registers 350°F (180°C) on a thermometer. Working in batches, fry the oysters, turning once during cooking, until they are golden brown, about a minute per side. (I love to lightly fry my oysters so that they are barely done, but feel free to cook them longer.) Transfer the oysters to a paper towel, season with sea salt, and add a squeeze of fresh lemon juice over the top. Serve hot with tartar sauce and additional lemon wedges, if desired.

THE HART

My grandmother, Dorothy Hart, spent her entire adult life teaching young women, and sometimes young men, how to cook and provide for their families as a home economics teacher. Cooking food was part of who she was: She spent countless hours standing over a hot stove providing food for family, friends, church members, holidays, funerals—or someone who just dropped by. As a kid, I wondered why she would constantly be sending my grandfather out on a food delivery to someone I didn't even know. But as I got older, I understood that food was her way of showing someone that she cared. When you were eating her food, you were family.

She never cooked with exotic ingredients or made overly complex sauces, but she did focus on fresh ingredients. There was no such thing as buying canned vegetables in her house. If you wanted canned vegetables in the winter, you better put them up yourself in the spring or summer! There was always substance to her food as well, what most people would call soul. I don't think she intended to cook food from the soul every day; it just seemed to happen. She also cooked from a place of love—from a pot of fresh peas to her legendary chocolate cake (which I must admit no one in the family has mastered). Before she passed, I always looked forward to her input on recipes I was working on. She'd try just about anything; she would admit to having two if she liked it; and if she really liked something, I'd eventually get the report back saying, "I ate the whole thing!" She also let me know when something didn't quite meet her expectations. She would never tell me it was bad or that she didn't like it. Instead, she would say, "It's good, but not exactly how I make mine."

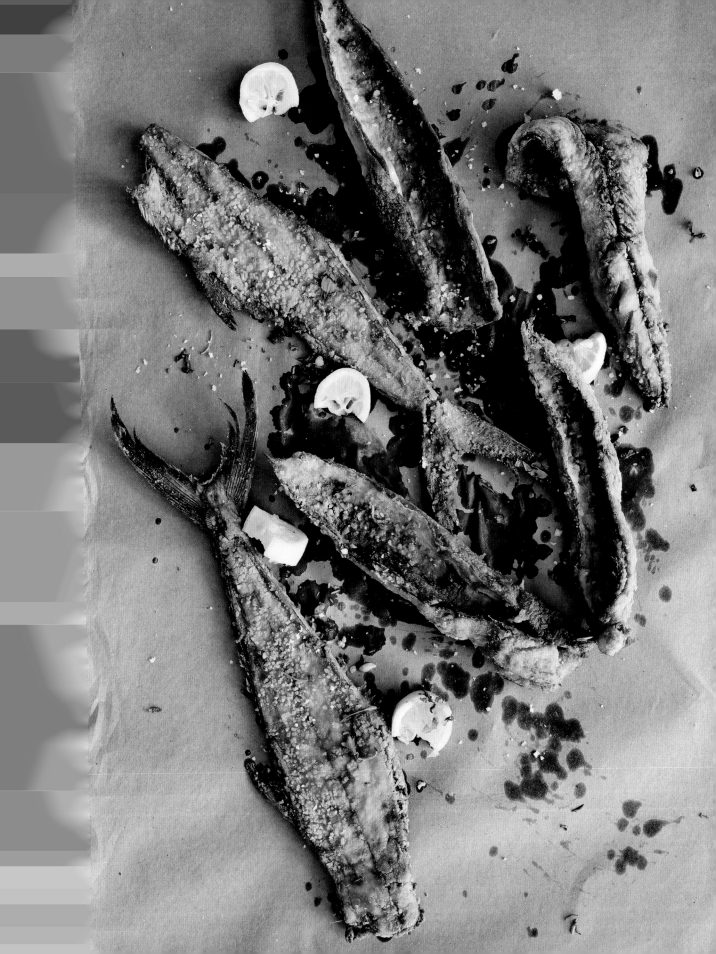

FRIED SPANISH MACKEREL HARP

Serves 6

2 whole Spanish mackerels, filleted (you will have 4 fillets and 2 harps)	½ cup (63 g) flour	Oil, for frying
	1 teaspoon garlic salt	Lemon wedges, for garnish
½ cup (120 ml) milk	2 teaspoons salt	Chopped parsley, for garnish
½ cup (70 g) cornmeal	1 teaspoon freshly ground black pepper	

During my early teens I spent a lot of time on a boat with my dad and my uncle, J.D. Gibson. We would take off early in the morning or late in the evening to chase Spanish mackerel along the inlet and edge of the surf. It's always satisfying to catch fish and have them cooking in hot grease just an hour or so later.

The unique thing about this recipe is the fact that it uses the whole fish. Most folks will fillet fish and throw away the middle part of the fillet. Uncle J.D. was a stickler for using the middle part of the fish, which he called the harp. I've come to agree with him that the middle part is often the sweetest and best part of the fish. Next time you're frying fish, sit back and let everyone else grab the fillets. Then you can have all the harp meat to yourself.

Note: Depending on the size of your fish, you may want to cut the fillets in half before breading and cooking. Don't cut the harps in half though.

Rinse the fillets under cold water and pat dry. Set aside. Pour the milk in a small shallow bowl and set aside. In a separate shallow bowl, mix the cornmeal and flour together until well combined. Lightly season each fish fillet with garlic salt, salt, and pepper.

In a large cast-iron skillet, add oil until it is ½ inch (1 cm) deep. Heat the oil over medium heat until a thermometer registers 375°F (190°C). Working in batches, add the fillets to the milk and then dredge them in the flour mixture until they are evenly coated. Carefully add the fillets to the hot oil—the grease will pop!—and fry for 3 to 4 minutes on each side, or until golden brown. Remove from the pan and set aside on a paper towel to drain.

Plate them up, then garnish with lemon wedges and parsley. Serve hot.

COLLARD CHOWDER

Serves 8 to 10

8 ounces (225 g) country ham, diced

1 large sweet onion, diced

2 tablespoons (28 g) salted butter

1 teaspoon ground turmeric

3 cups (710 ml) collard stock (below)

3 cups (330 g) diced potatoes

3 cups (540 g) cooked collards (below)

1 cup (235 ml) heavy cream

1 teaspoon freshly ground black pepper

The idea for collard chowder was partly inspired by clam chowder, one of my favorite cool-weather treats . . . but also by thrift. I desperately wanted to find a recipe that could make the most of the extra cooking liquid that normally goes down the drain after cooking huge piles of collards. Just like clam chowder, this soup features heavy cream and potatoes. However, clams and collards are not a classic combination! Instead, I switched out the protein for the classic collard companion: country ham. From there it was a matter of dialing in the spices. I originally tried it as a spicy soup, featuring cayenne. However, I eventually realized this soup was more delicious with a mixture of turmeric and black pepper.

In a large stockpot, cook the ham over medium heat until it starts to brown, about 3 minutes. Add the onion and butter to the pot. When the onion starts to become translucent, add the turmeric and stir. Add the collard stock and potatoes and cook until the potatoes are tender, about 5 minutes.

Add the collards, heavy cream, and pepper. Give the pot a good stir. Cook the chowder for an additional 8 to 10 minutes, stirring occasionally. Serve hot with a slice of cornbread.

COLLARDS AND STOCK

Makes 3 cups collard greens and 4 cups stock

2½ pounds (1 kg) collard greens, coarsely chopped

1 tablespoon (18 g) salt

6 cups (1.4 l) water

If you don't have collards already cooked, this is a basic recipe to get the stock and cooked collards you'll need for the chowder. This isn't how I normally cook them (see page 148 for that), but it's easy enough and works perfectly for the flavor of the chowder.

In a 10-quart (9.4 l) stockpot over medium heat, combine the collards, salt, and water. Cook, stirring occasionally, for an hour, or until the collards are tender but not mushy. Drain, reserving the stock.

LENOIR COUNTY FISH STEW

Serves 10

10 slices bacon

½ cup (120 ml) white wine

18 ounces (510 g) tomato paste

3 tablespoons (30 g) minced garlic

2 tablespoons red pepper flakes
  (or more if you want a spicier soup)

5 pounds (2.3 kg) white potatoes,
  sliced into ¼-inch (0.5 cm) rounds

2 pounds (905 g) white fish
  (such as catfish or flounder),
  cut into 3-inch (7.5 cm) pieces

3 pounds (1.4 kg) white onions,
  sliced into rings

½ cup (30 g) fresh parsley

2 teaspoons salt, plus additional to taste

½ teaspoon freshly ground black pepper

2 bay leaves

10 eggs (or 1 for each serving)

It seems that this style of fish stew is found in areas between Goldsboro and Kinston, North Carolina, with recipes being passed down through the generations. Every family has their little tweak in how they do it. In my family, my grandfather, who grew up in Lenoir County, was the chef behind the family recipe. Of course, it wasn't written down. To decode this recipe, I had to make it time and again, being told to add just a little bit of this or less of that. I'm happy to say that I eventually got my Gran's seal of approval.

This isn't a thick soup; however, the light broth is full of flavor with a bit of heat on the end. The heartiness comes from the loads of fish and potatoes—somewhat like a classic Mediterranean fisherman's stew. Fish stew should be enjoyed with a crowd of people. Just make sure you have at least one egg for every person who will be eating it. It also should be served with plain white loaf bread so that you can sop up the broth in the bottom of the bowl.

In a large stockpot, fry the bacon over medium heat until crispy. Remove the bacon from the grease and set aside. Add the white wine to the bacon grease, scraping any bits of bacon off the bottom of the pot, and cook for 1 minute. With a wooden spoon, stir the tomato paste into the wine mixture. Add the garlic and red pepper flakes, mix well, and cook for 2 minutes.

Turn off the heat and remove the pot from the stove. Layer the potatoes, fish, and onions in the pot, starting with a layer of potatoes. Lay down enough potatoes to cover the bottom of the pot, but leave a little room on the sides. Then layer in a few pieces of fish, followed by a layer of onions—just enough to cover the fish. Repeat this process until all the ingredients are used, then add the parsley on top. (Depending on the size of your pot, the number of layers will vary slightly.)

(continued)

Over the last layer of onions, add the salt, black pepper, and bay leaves.

Fill the pot with filtered water so that it covers the top layer by ¼ inch (0.5 cm). Place the lid on the pot and bring the soup to a boil over medium heat. Reduce the heat to a simmer. Cook for 10 minutes, or until the potatoes are almost done. Crack the eggs over the top of the broth. Once the eggs are cooked through, taste the broth and add more salt if needed. Remove and discard the bay leaves.

Portion out the stew in bowls, making sure each bowl has plenty of fish and potatoes and at least one egg. Serve hot with a slice of white bread.

EASTERN NORTH CAROLINA WHITE SLAW *(pictured on page 66)*

Serves 6

1 medium head green cabbage	1 tablespoon (18 g) salt	1 cup (225 g) Duke's Mayonnaise
5 carrots	½ teaspoon coarsely ground black pepper	(page 54)
½ cup (100 g) sugar	¼ cup (60 ml) white vinegar	

Hot dogs and mustard, tacos and cilantro, hamburgers and cheese: Classic combinations are established for a reason. Some foods just don't seem complete without that magical pairing. For me, and for countless others, barbecue just isn't complete without a helping of slaw. The crisp side dish perfectly cuts through the richness of the meat.

In North Carolina, we have two distinct types of slaw in the eastern and western parts of the state (sound familiar?). In the eastern half of the state, we have a white slaw that is mayonnaise based. In the western side of the state, there's a red ketchup–based slaw instead. Having grown up in the eastern part of the state, I use this white slaw with the pulled pork on page 42 (and it pairs equally well with fried seafood). Naturally, this is a family recipe, though it doesn't go quite as far back as some of the others. My mom's slaw has never been beat, and the secret is one you can copy: Make sure you use Duke's Mayonnaise.

Using a box grater, grate the entire head of cabbage and transfer to a large mixing bowl. Then grate the carrots and add them to the bowl. You should have about 7½ cups (525 g) of cabbage and 1 cup (110 g) of carrots once you shred them.

Sprinkle the sugar, salt, and pepper over the cabbage and carrots. Pour the vinegar over the top and lightly toss the mixture with your hands to make sure all ingredients are well combined. Add the mayonnaise and toss the mixture with a spoon until the vegetables are uniformly coated. Refrigerate until ready to serve.

(continued)

WESTERN NORTH CAROLINA RED SLAW *(not pictured)*

Serves 6

¾ cup (180 g) ketchup

½ cup (120 ml) apple cider vinegar

½ cup (100 g) sugar

1 teaspoon hot sauce

2 teaspoons salt

2 teaspoons freshly ground
   black pepper

1 medium head cabbage,
   finely chopped

While I'm an eastern slaw kind of guy, western slaw has plenty of fans. Plus, if you're making a spread of western-style pork, you might as well have the slaw that's supposed to go with it, right?

In a large mixing bowl, whisk together the ketchup, vinegar, sugar, hot sauce, salt, and pepper. Add the cabbage and stir until it is uniformly coated. Refrigerate for at least 20 minutes and serve chilled.

◄ Eastern North Carolina White Slaw (page 65)

MAC AND CHEESE

Serves 6 to 8

½ cup (1 stick, 112 g) salted butter

2 cloves garlic, minced

1 cup (125 g) flour

1 quart (946 ml) heavy cream

1 tablespoon dried oregano

1 pound (455 g) penne pasta

3 cups (345 g) shredded sharp
Cheddar cheese

2 cups (225 g) shredded mild
Cheddar cheese

Southern Smoke can be extra busy on Fridays, and the odd thing is that it's usually not for a barbecue special—it's mac and cheese that's the draw. Maybe that's because this recipe goes far above what passes for mac and cheese at many restaurants these days. We start ours out with a lot of butter, flour, and garlic—almost like a classic French béchamel sauce. Then we slowly add sharp Cheddar cheese as the cream begins to boil. After we mix the noodles and cream sauce together, we finish the dish by topping with mild Cheddar. The ridges in the penne pasta catch the melted cheese and cream, so every bite is perfectly loaded with cheese.

Preheat the oven to 400°F (200°C). Bring a large stockpot of salted water to a boil over high heat.

Meanwhile, in a 3-quart (2.8 l) saucepan over medium heat, melt the butter. Add the garlic and cook until it becomes aromatic, about 30 seconds. Add the flour and stir until the mixture becomes light brown, about 3 minutes.

Slowly add the heavy cream. Whisk the mixture together slowly until it begins to thicken. Add the oregano, reduce the heat to low, and allow the mixture to simmer.

Add the pasta to the boiling water and cook for 8 minutes, or until it is almost al dente.

While the pasta is boiling, slowly stir the sharp Cheddar into the simmering cream mixture. The mixture should become very thick and creamy.

When the pasta is finished, drain it in a colander. Pour the cooked pasta into a 2-quart (1.9 l) casserole dish. Slowly pour the cream and cheese mixture over the top of the pasta. With a large spoon, stir the mixture until all of the pasta is well coated. Top the mixture with the mild Cheddar cheese. Bake for 5 minutes, or until the cheese is golden brown and bubbly.

SQUASH AND RICE PUDDING

Serves 8

2 tablespoons (28 g) butter

2 pounds (905 g) yellow squash,
  cut into ¼-inch (0.5 cm) slices

2 teaspoons salt, divided

3 cups (585 g) uncooked white rice

2 cups (460 g) sour cream

2 cups (475 ml) heavy cream

1 tablespoon chopped fresh basil

1 teaspoon chopped fresh oregano

1 teaspoon coarsely ground black pepper

The first sign that summer is around the corner is when our farmers switch from dropping off greens to dropping off squash. By May, our squash farmer is making frequent trips from his farm just a few miles down the road to drop off 20-pound (9 kg) boxes. At some point, the excitement of fresh squash turns to the question of what to do with all of it. . . .

This recipe was inspired by a classic rice pudding from the Women's Cookery Cookbook, *published in 1914. Because the base for the pudding is quite soupy, I decided that it was a perfect fit for summer squash. No water is needed in addition to the sour cream and heavy cream. Fresh summer squash releases all the extra cooking liquid you'll need. I punch it up with lots of fresh basil and a touch of oregano, and fresh is key. Feel free to play with the herbs in your garden, or top with even more basil. This should be a dish that screams summer, despite it being a hot rice casserole.*

Preheat the oven to 350°F (180°C). In a large saucepan over medium heat, melt the butter. Add the squash and cook for 15 minutes, or until very tender (actually a bit mushy). Let the squash cool in the pan; do not drain off the liquid.

While the squash cools, start the rice. In a medium pot, bring 5½ cups (1.3 l) of water to a boil. Add 1 teaspoon of the salt and the rice. Cover the pot and return to a boil. Reduce the heat to a simmer and cook, covered, for 18 minutes, or until the rice is tender. If the rice is not done but it's getting dry, add more water and continue to cook until the rice is fully cooked and tender.

Pour the cooked rice into a 2-quart (1.9 l) casserole dish. Add the cooked squash and juices to the rice, then fold in the sour cream, heavy cream, basil, oregano, the remaining 1 teaspoon salt, and the pepper. Stir until completely mixed.

Cover the baking dish with foil and bake for 20 minutes. Uncover and bake for an additional 10 minutes, or until the edges begin to brown.

BROWN BUTTER CREAMED CORN

Serves 4

½ cup (1 stick, 112 g) salted butter

8 ears fresh corn

1¼ cups (285 ml) heavy cream

3 cloves garlic, minced

2 tablespoons chopped fresh basil

2 tablespoons (26 g) sugar

½ tablespoon freshly ground
  black pepper

Corn represents the official halfway point of summer to me as it tends to come into the restaurant right around the Fourth of July. It's not only at every potluck this time of year, but we also put it up. For country folk, putting up corn—preserving it for later—is no small task. Most people pick up 15 to 20 dozen ears of corn. As a group, everyone works to shuck it, get the silk off, sash it, cream it, and then freeze it in plastic bags.

Why go through all the work? I can tell you, there's just something special about being able to enjoy the taste and smell of fresh creamed corn on a Sunday in January. No canned product tastes quite like it. If you do the same, follow my grandmother's advice and mark the bags with where the corn was from and the date it was bagged.

This recipe for creamed corn is different from the one I grew up on, which was very sweet. I tried instead to let the sweetness of the corn shine through and complement it with the nutty, salty flavor of brown butter. Lots of fresh basil amps up the feeling of summer.

In a 4-quart (3.8 l) pot over medium heat, melt the butter and then brown it. The butter will go through distinct stages, foaming and turning from lemon yellow to tan. Finally, it will turn brown and give off a nutty aroma. At this point, remove it from the heat and set it aside (it's a good idea to refrigerate it to stop the cooking process, if you can).

Cut the corn kernels from the cobs with a small paring knife and collect them in a large mixing bowl. Once the kernels have been removed, use the back of the knife blade and scrape along the cob to get the milky liquid out of the cob and into the mixing bowl. Set the bowl aside. You can discard all the cobs at this point except one. Cut the reserved cob in half to use like a soup bone.

Transfer the cob halves to a small pot and add the heavy cream. Cook over medium heat until the cream begins to slowly boil, about 4 minutes. Immediately remove the pot from the heat and set aside.

Place the pot with the brown butter back on the stove over medium heat. If the butter solidified in the fridge, melt it again, then add the garlic, cut corn, basil, sugar, and pepper and stir until well combined. Cook for 1 minute.

Remove the corncob halves from the heavy cream and slowly add the cream to the corn mixture. Stir until the mixture is uniform and reduce the heat to medium-low. Cook for 30 minutes, stirring periodically to prevent burning. The mixture will begin to thicken and become creamy as it cooks.

PORK BELLY AND SWEET POTATO HASH

Serves 6

4 medium sweet potatoes	1 tablespoon ground cinnamon	2 tablespoons chopped fresh parsley
2 pounds (905 g) pork belly	¼ teaspoon ground ginger	Pinch of sea salt
2 tablespoons (30 g) packed brown sugar	¼ teaspoon ground nutmeg	

North Carolina may be best known for its pork, but we grow a lot of sweet potatoes as well (see page 182). This recipe was one I came up with as an homage to these local favorites. The inspiration was actually the rich, fatty pork belly from Heritage Farms Cheshire Pork and the superlative sweet potatoes from Buch Farms. There's no need to special order though—just use the best-quality meat and sweet potatoes you can find.

The warm flavors of this fall dish were a hit beyond my wildest dreams: sweet and salty, like a warm pumpkin pie mixed with the deep, rich flavor of pork belly. This recipe eventually caught the attention of the Today Show, *and I ended up onstage cooking with Al Roker! However, Al's not the recipe's most important fan—this is my lovely wife's favorite dish as well.*

Preheat the oven to 350°F (180°C). Dice the sweet potatoes into ½-inch (1 cm) pieces. (You should have 3 cups [330 g] of diced sweet potatoes.) Transfer the potatoes to a 3-quart casserole dish, cover with foil, and roast for 30 minutes, or until tender but not completely fork-tender. Set the potatoes aside and turn off the oven.

Cut the pork belly into 1-inch (2.5 cm) pieces. (You should have about 2 cups [280 g].) In a 10-inch (25 cm) nonstick skillet over medium heat, cook the pork belly for about 5 minutes, or until it starts to brown. Add the brown sugar and sweet potatoes. Continue cooking for 4 minutes more, or until the sweet potatoes become fork-tender. Add the cinnamon, ginger, nutmeg, parsley, and sea salt. Stir to combine and cook for 2 minutes more before serving.

CORNMEAL FRIED OKRA

Serves 4

2 to 3 tablespoons (30 to 45 ml)
    vegetable oil

3 cups (860 g) sliced fresh okra,
    cut into ¼-inch [0.5 cm] pieces

½ teaspoon paprika

¼ teaspoon freshly ground black pepper

½ cup (70 g) yellow cornmeal

½ teaspoon salt, or more to taste

When most people picture fried okra, they think of the heavily battered fried okra that is seen in restaurants across the United States. This recipe is more of an "old school" version of the dish. It doesn't use any egg wash or batter, and you don't even have to use a deep fryer. You essentially cook the okra in a small amount of oil and lightly dust it with cornmeal. (If you want, you can really crank up the flavor when it's finished by sprinkling on a little Cajun seasoning or cayenne pepper.) It's quite easy to make and also a bit healthier than heavily breaded and fried versions that drip with grease. I think it even makes a great alternative to french fries when you're having a burger or a steak.

In a large cast-iron skillet, heat the vegetable oil over medium-high heat, making sure you have enough oil to completely cover the bottom of the pan. When the oil is hot enough that cornmeal sizzles when sprinkled in, add all the okra to the pan. Sprinkle the okra with the paprika and pepper and stir with a wooden spoon. Cook for 1 minute, then sprinkle the cornmeal over the entire pan of okra and stir until each piece of okra is coated. Cook for an additional 4 minutes, or until the okra is golden brown. Transfer the okra to a paper towel to drain. While the okra is still hot, season with salt and serve.

Note: It's important that you don't add salt until the okra is completely cooked. If you add salt to the okra early, it will pull moisture out and make the okra soggy. With this recipe, you are looking for a crunchy bite of okra.

BBQ POTATOES

5 pounds (2.3 kg) Yukon gold potatoes,
   peeled and diced

½ cup (1 stick, 112 g) salted butter,
   cut into ¼-inch (0.5 cm) pieces

¼ cup (60 ml) hot sauce

1 cup (250 g) Western North Carolina BBQ
   Sauce (page 45)

½ cup (120 ml) Eastern North Carolina
   Vinegar Sauce (page 44)

1½ teaspoons salt

1 teaspoon freshly ground black pepper

First things first: The name of this recipe is a little misleading for the uninitiated. BBQ Potatoes aren't smoked—they aren't even cooked on a grill. However, don't let that stop you from trying this recipe as these potatoes are delicious.

Barbecue restaurants in many parts of eastern North Carolina still serve these potatoes family-style, alongside overflowing bowls of fried chicken, slaw, and BBQ pork. The potatoes vary a bit from place to place, but generally they're cooked in the oven in a mixture of butter and the restaurant's house sweet BBQ sauce. For this recipe, I follow those general rules but recommend a hit of hot sauce and vinegar sauce for a more complex flavor. Try serving these at your next cookout to round out a plate of meat and slaw.

Preheat the oven to 400°F (200°C). Place the potatoes in a 2-quart (1.9 l) casserole dish. Scatter the pieces of butter over the top of the potatoes.

In a mixing bowl, combine the hot sauce, BBQ sauce, and vinegar sauce. Pour the sauce mixture over the potatoes. Season the potatoes with the salt and pepper. Stir everything together with a large spoon until all of the potatoes are coated evenly.

Cover the dish with foil and bake for 30 minutes. Remove the potatoes from the oven and give them a quick stir. If the potatoes look a little dry when you stir them, you can add up to ½ cup (120 ml) of water. Place the foil back over top and cook for an additional 15 minutes, or until the potatoes are tender. Serve hot from the oven if you can!

BRAISED CABBAGE WITH BACON AND WHITE WINE

Serves 4

5 slices bacon, finely diced

1 clove garlic, minced

1 tablespoon (15 ml) lemon juice

⅓ cup (80 ml) white wine

1 medium head cabbage (about 2 pounds [905 g]), chopped

1 teaspoon salt

½ teaspoon freshly ground black pepper

With a pastor for a father, of course my family has a strong tradition of gathering after church for Sunday lunch. Braised cabbage has long been one of my grandmother's standout dishes for these lunches (though as a Southern Baptist, she wouldn't dare keep wine in the house). My version is not as shy about the wine, though it is a modest addition. With this recipe, you'll end up with a flavorful pot of stewed cabbage that, together with the bacon, is both salty and silky.

In a large pot over medium heat, cook the bacon. When the bacon begins to brown, add the garlic and stir until it becomes aromatic, about 10 seconds. Add the lemon juice and stir to keep the garlic from burning, then add the wine and let cook for 1 minute.

Add ½ cup (120 ml) of water, the cabbage, salt, and pepper and stir everything together. Reduce the heat to medium-low. Place a lid on the pot and simmer for 20 to 25 minutes, or until the cabbage is very tender.

THE LOW COUNTRY

Shrimp, Rice, and Okra

There are few places where culture and food have been shaped by their location more than the Low Country. The rich coastal waters from Charleston to the Brunswick, Georgia, islands have served as a source of nutrition and income for centuries. For all its beauty and bounty, not all things that are associated with this part of the world are wonderful. This area, like much of the South, was shaped by people who didn't come here by choice. The culinary influence of West African slaves on the cuisine of the Low Country is truly remarkable. The fingerprints of regions such as Sierra Leone are stamped throughout the region. Under beautiful oak trees draped with Spanish moss, families and friends have gathered around dinner tables to celebrate the bounties of the Low Country for centuries. Unique flavors can be found all over this region—from its fine dining restaurants in Charleston and Savannah to the back-road seafood shacks that dot its coastline.

SMOKED AND FRIED CHICKEN WINGS WITH MUSTARD-BASED BBQ SAUCE

Serves 4

For the Mustard-Based BBQ Sauce

1½ cups (355 ml) apple cider vinegar

1½ cups (265 g) yellow mustard

½ cup (120 g) ketchup

⅓ cup (75 g) packed brown sugar

1 tablespoon (18 g) salt

1 teaspoon freshly ground black pepper

1 tablespoon (18 g) garlic salt

2 teaspoons corn syrup

1 teaspoon red pepper flakes

For the Wings

4 pounds (1.8 kg) chicken wings

   (separated into wings and drumettes)

3 tablespoons (54 g) salt

3 tablespoons (18 g) freshly ground

   black pepper

5½ tablespoons (39 g) paprika

Canola oil, for frying

1 cup (170 g) Mustard-Based BBQ Sauce,

   plus additional sauce for serving

While the Low Country isn't famous for any particular smoked meat, it is known for a particular sauce. Mustard-based barbecue sauces are very much a regional passion, with the strongest mustard belt running from Columbia to Charleston. If we look to history, this affinity for mustard likely came in with the Germans. In the 1730s to 1750s, the British colony of South Carolina actively recruited and encouraged families in Germany to come and settle in that region. Many families were given land grants in the region as an incentive. Vinegar-based sauce was already being used in the region for smoked meats, but in search of a small taste of home, the Germans introduced mustard into the mix. Nearly 300 years later, the sauce remains as popular as ever.

Naturally, those in other regions beg to differ. Here in eastern North Carolina, I've heard judgmental friends say, "They put that mustard sauce on their BBQ down there!" like it's a bad thing. I admit, in my younger years I may have thought the same thing. However, my friend Bryan Furman of B's Cracklin' BBQ in Savannah (and now Atlanta) changed my mind. His sauce blew me away with its balance of tangy and sweet; I had to agree it went perfectly with the platter of smoked meats in front of me.

When I returned from that trip, I dove into recipe development, and the result is the sauce you see here. You'll find it goes well with most meats and also doubles as a fine dipping sauce for french fries. I like it so much I even serve it from time to time here in vinegar-based country. You never know—I could convert a few locals!

(continued)

To make the sauce: In a mixing bowl, combine all the sauce ingredients and stir until well combined. Transfer the sauce to an airtight container and store in the refrigerator while making the wings, or for at least an hour before serving if using for another recipe. This sauce will last about 14 days in the fridge.

To make the wings: Prepare a grill for smoking (see page 25). Pat the wings dry and season them liberally with the salt, pepper, and paprika. Smoke the wings over indirect heat for about 1½ hours, or until the wings register an internal temperature of 140°F (60°C).

About 20 minutes before the wings are done, preheat your deep fryer to 350°F (180°C) or heat at least 3 cups of canola oil in a heavy-bottomed Dutch oven until it reaches 350°F (180°C). When the wings reach 140°F (60°C), remove them from the smoker. Working in batches so as not to crowd the deep fryer or Dutch oven, fry the wings for 3 to 5 minutes, or until they reach 160°F (70°C). Transfer the cooked wings to a large heatproof bowl. Lightly toss the wings with 1 cup of the BBQ sauce until all the wings are coated. Serve immediately with additional sauce on the side.

COUNTRY CAPTAIN CHICKEN

Serves 6

1 pound (455 g) boneless, skinless chicken breasts, cut into ¾-inch (2 cm) pieces

1½ teaspoons paprika

1 teaspoon salt, plus more to taste

1 teaspoon freshly ground black pepper, plus more to taste

1 cup flour

½ cup (120 ml) canola oil

3 tablespoons (42 g) butter

2 cups (300 g) sliced onions

2 cups (300 g) diced bell peppers

2 cloves garlic, minced

2 teaspoons curry powder

1 cup (145 g) golden raisins

1 can (28 ounces [794 g]) diced tomatoes

1 tablespoon dried thyme

1½ tablespoons chopped parsley

½ cup (55 g) slivered almonds

4 cups (660 g) cooked rice, for serving

How did an Indian dish, cooked by a Swedish chef from New York City, that was loved by a former president, become a Southern icon? For the complicated story behind this dish, see page 89. On the flavor front, what you need to know is that there's a reason Country Captain Chicken has been popular for decades. Anytime you begin a recipe with frying chicken, you will get the attention of most Southerners. When you add in the element of garlic and tomatoes, with the sweetness of raisins, and throw in the distinct flavor of curry powder, you get a real crowd-pleaser. The longer you simmer your fried chicken in the sauce, the deeper the flavors will penetrate the chicken—and the more tender your chicken will become.

Season the chicken with the paprika, salt, and black pepper. Add the flour to a bowl and dredge the chicken in the flour until well coated. Shake off any excess flour.

In a Dutch oven, heat the oil over medium-high heat. Once the oil begins to shimmer, cook the chicken in batches until browned on both sides, about 8 minutes. Set the chicken aside after frying.

Drain off any excess oil, leaving about a tablespoon in the Dutch oven. Reduce the heat to low, then add the butter and let it melt. Add the onions, bell peppers, and garlic. Increase the heat to medium and cook for 4 minutes, stirring occasionally to prevent burning. Add the curry powder and raisins, stir, and cook for about 1 minute before adding the tomatoes, thyme, parsley, and almonds. Bring the mixture to a simmer, then return the chicken to the pot. Cook, stirring occasionally, for 35 minutes, or until the chicken is tender. Add salt and pepper to taste.

To serve, spoon the chicken and gravy over cooked rice and serve hot.

COUNTRY CAPTAIN

There are many stories that swirl around the evolution of the "Country Captain." Some say the dish was brought into one of the Low Country ports, either Charleston or Savannah, by a sea captain traveling from India. This seems reasonable, as the dish features Indian flavors and techniques and eventually was best known in the Low Country. However, the first publication I've been able to track down was in the *International Cookbook*, published in 1905, and attributed to a Swiss-born chef at Delmonico's in New York City, Alessandro Filippini.

Whether it originated in Charleston or New York, the dish ended up being popularized by Mary Bullard, the wife of a prominent physician in Columbus, Georgia. She served her version of the dish at social gatherings to rave reviews. At the time, curry powder was not a readily available ingredient, and she further distinguished the dish by adding tomatoes as the chicken cooked.

The Bullard family had a summer home in nearby Warm Springs, where one of their neighbors was Franklin Delano Roosevelt, who was recovering from polio. He quickly fell in love with the dish, and rumor was that it became a lifelong favorite.

After the Second World War, Country Captain began appearing prominently in *Charleston Receipts*, a book published in the 1950s by the Charleston Junior League. It soon became a standard for home cooks. While it is somewhat time-consuming, it is easy to pull off, and the rich tomato gravy is a wintertime treat.

SHRIMP AND GRITS

Serves 4

For the Grits

2 cups (475 ml) heavy cream

2 cups (475 ml) whole milk

¾ teaspoon salt

1 cup (148 g) stone-ground grits

For the Shrimp

3 tablespoons (42 g) butter

2 cups (140 g) sliced mushrooms

2 cloves garlic, minced

1 pound (455 g) shrimp, peeled
  and deveined

1 cup (100 g) sliced green onions

Splash of white wine

¼ cup (60 ml) lemon juice

Hot sauce, such as Texas Pete, to taste

½ cup (120 ml) heavy cream

Salt and freshly ground black pepper

2 tablespoons chopped fresh parsley,
  for garnish

When you think of dishes that represent a region, Shrimp and Grits has to be the dish that represents the Low Country. Various recipes have been around since the American Indians, and you can find references to the iconic dish in Gullah cooking, but it has not been a Low Country staple for as long as you may think.

Its quick rise to stardom began after Craig Claiborne wrote a stirring review of Chef Bill Neal's shrimp and grits at Crook's Corner in 1985. From this one review, the dish spread like wildfire. Now it can be found in back-road dives, local mom-and-pop restaurants, and some of the finest restaurants in Charleston— and across America. While chefs from all over have created delicious riffs on the classic, one thing is not negotiable: You must start with fresh shrimp and high-quality grits.

The recipe here is classic and delicious as written. However, this is a recipe you can modify to suit your tastes as well. Adding cheese to the grits brings another layer of flavor to the dish (start with about 1½ cups shredded [180 g]). You can also play around with the shrimp mixture—adding fresh corn or bell pepper, for example. Last but not least, crumbled bacon makes for a fine garnish!

(continued)

To make the grits: In a medium saucepan over high heat, bring the heavy cream, milk, and salt to a boil. Slowly pour in the grits. Reduce the heat to medium and cook, stirring constantly, for 10 minutes, or until the grits thicken. Once the grits become creamy and thick, remove the pan from the heat and cover it while you prepare the shrimp.

To make the shrimp: In a large nonstick pan over medium heat, melt the butter. Add the mushrooms and cook, stirring occasionally, for 3 to 4 minutes, or until they have begun to reduce in size. Add the garlic and cook for 1 minute. Add the shrimp and green onions and cook for 3 minutes, stirring enough to prevent burning. Add the white wine and lemon juice to deglaze the bottom of the pan, then cook for 1 minute. Add the hot sauce, if desired, and give the mixture a quick stir. Add the heavy cream and let the mixture simmer for 2 to 3 minutes, then season with salt and pepper to taste.

As the shrimp finishes cooking, or once it's done, you can divide the grits among serving bowls or plates. Spoon the shrimp mixture over the top of the grits and garnish with fresh parsley. Serve immediately.

PICKLED SHRIMP

(pictured on page 94)

Serves 6 as an appetizer

1 pound (455 g) shrimp, peeled and deveined	½ teaspoon sea salt	¼ cup (15 g) fresh parsley
½ cup (120 ml) olive oil	½ teaspoon red pepper flakes	3 cloves garlic
⅓ cup (80 ml) lemon juice	½ teaspoon peppercorns	1 medium onion, cut in half and sliced thin
	5 dill sprigs	1 lemon, cut in half and sliced

Seafood is a point of pride in the Low Country. The rich waters of the tidal estuaries along the coast of South Carolina and Georgia have provided families with a source of nutrition and income for hundreds of years. While there's no official favorite, shrimp is the most well-known product that is harvested from the waters. Three types of shrimp can be found in the coastal waters: roe shrimp (harvested in May to June), Brown's shrimp (harvested from June to August), and white shrimp (harvested from August to December).

Thinking of shrimp like this, with harvest dates, helps many people understand why you'd pickle it. There are specific times shrimp is at its freshest. If you can't eat them all immediately, pickling them is the next best thing.

Pickled shrimp have actually been around forever, because in the South we will pretty much pickle everything! I love adding lots of dill and garlic to fresh summertime Brown's shrimp and then giving them a good week to marinate. It's a great beach or lake snack: Drop a jar in a cooler along with your favorite beverages and break them out on a hot summer day.

Bring 2 quarts (1.9 l) of salted water to a boil. Add the shrimp and cook for 3 to 5 minutes, or until the shrimp are pink. Drain the shrimp in a colander and rinse under cold water to stop cooking. Set the shrimp aside.

In a metal bowl, whisk the olive oil and lemon juice together. Add the sea salt, red pepper flakes, peppercorns, dill sprigs, parsley, and garlic and whisk to combine. In a quart Mason jar, layer the shrimp, onion, and lemon in each jar until they are ¼ inch (0.5 cm) from the top. Add the olive oil mixture to the jar, then secure the airtight lid. Refrigerate for at least 3 days to let the flavors meld (a week works best). They will last for a few weeks.

SOUTH CAROLINA SHRIMP

The coastal estuaries and waters of South Carolina are home to numerous varieties of shrimp. The two most common shrimp that are found in these waters are the brown and white shrimp. Because of the abundance of shrimp in the region, it has become one of the most prized natural resources. Each type of shrimp is harvested at different times of the year; white shrimp are normally harvested in May and June, while browns are usually harvested from June to August. As shrimp grow in size, they leave the brackish waters of the tidal pools and move toward the higher salinity levels of the open ocean. The biggest difference in the two shrimp is when it comes to feeding. When white shrimp are in staging areas, they will move into the shallow estuaries to feed at night, while brown shrimp will stay in the deep waters and not feed at night. The average shrimp size is usually 6 inches, but in years when there is an abundance of shrimp in the tidal pools and excessive rainfall, young shrimp are pushed from shallow waters because of low salinity, so shrimp size will be smaller. Luckily, because of warm winters and variable weather, fresh shrimp can be enjoyed almost eight months out of the year in the Low Country.

◄ Pickled Shrimp (page 93)

JAMES ISLAND SHRIMP PIE

Serves 8

1 cup (195 g) uncooked rice

2 cups (475 ml) water

2 teaspoons salt

4 tablespoons (55 g) butter

1 small onion, diced

1 green bell pepper, diced

2 cloves garlic

2 tablespoons (30 ml)
  Worcestershire sauce

2 pounds (905 g) peeled and
  deveined medium shrimp

Salt and freshly ground black pepper
  to taste

1 cup (235 ml) heavy cream

2 large eggs, beaten

1 tablespoon flour

1 large tomato, sliced

1½ cups (165 g) bread crumbs

The South is full of old Junior League cookbooks. I often turn to them as a source of inspiration, as they let me look back into the kitchens of women from decades past—showing me what they cooked for the people they loved. One of my favorites among these books is called Charleston Receipts, *published by the Junior League of Charleston in 1950. In this book, you will find a recipe for "James Island Shrimp Pie," submitted by Mrs. John T. Jenkins (though she credits an original recipe she got from Mrs. Robert Lebby Sr. that dates back to 1860!). The original recipe called for ketchup and mace, which we omitted. Instead, we use fresh sliced tomatoes along with bell peppers and onions to add a little crunch and flavor.*

In a small pot, combine the rice, water, and salt and cook over medium heat until very soft, about 25 minutes.

Once the rice is ready, you can start the rest of the recipe. Grease a 9 × 9-inch (23 × 23 cm) baking dish and set aside. Preheat the oven to 325°F (170°C).

In a large skillet over medium heat, melt the butter. Add the onion and bell pepper and cook until the onion is translucent, about 5 minutes. Add the garlic and Worcestershire sauce and stir until the garlic becomes aromatic. Add the shrimp and cook until pink, about 3 minutes, stirring to prevent burning. Season to taste with salt and black pepper. Remove the pan from the burner.

In a heatproof mixing bowl, combine the cooked rice, shrimp mixture, heavy cream, eggs, and flour. Stir until well combined; it should have a custardlike thickness.

Pour the mixture into the baking dish. Place the tomato slices over the top of the rice and shrimp mixture, making sure not to layer them. Sprinkle the bread crumbs over the top of the tomatoes. Bake for 25 minutes, or until bubbly and golden brown.

SMOKED SHRIMP

Serves 4

2 pounds (905 g) shrimp, headed and
deveined, shell on (see note)

3 tablespoons (45 ml) olive oil

1½ teaspoons dried oregano

1 teaspoon garlic salt

1 teaspoon salt

2 teaspoons paprika

1½ teaspoons sugar

½ teaspoon freshly ground black pepper

Lime wedges, for serving

Smoked shrimp is incredibly versatile; its ability to add a unique flavor to lots of dishes is simply amazing. There is no better way to spice up a pasta dish or a plain cheese quesadilla than with these smoked shrimp. They also can be made ahead and stored in the refrigerator for a quick topping for that boring salad the next day for lunch.

In a large bowl, toss the shrimp with the olive oil. Sprinkle the oregano, garlic salt, salt, paprika, sugar, and pepper over the top of the shrimp. Lightly mix the shrimp together with your hands to ensure the shrimp are evenly coated with the rub. Prepare a smoker according to the directions on page 25. Set your smoker to 225°F (107°C). If you are using large shrimp, you can place them directly on your smoker grate; if not, you can place a piece of foil over the area you will be using, making sure you don't cover your fire. Smoke the shrimp until they are pink, about 30 minutes. Serve hot with lemon wedges.

Note: I like to leave the shell on the shrimp because that way, you get only a hint of smoke, which accentuates the flavor of the shrimp. If you want a heavy smoke flavor, peeling the shrimp is the way to go. Using a fruit wood such as apple or cherry goes very nicely with the shrimp.

SHRIMP AND OKRA

Serves 6

5 tablespoons (75 ml) olive oil	1 pound (455 g) shrimp, peeled and deveined	2 pounds [905 g] okra, diced
1 cup (150 g) sliced red onion	1 tablespoon chopped fresh thyme	Salt to taste
1 teaspoon red pepper flakes	1 tablespoon chopped fresh basil	Freshly ground black pepper to taste
3 cloves garlic, minced		

Okra is a staple in the Gullah/Geechee cuisine that is found across the Low Country (see page 108), which makes sense because it is one of the crops imported to the South from Africa. Okra is easy to grow and performs well in coastal climates. Because shrimp is also plentiful on the coast, the pairing of the two was inevitable. This is a satisfying one-pot meal that combines two of the Low Country's most abundant resources. Serve it in the summer when okra is at its peak and shrimp are easy to find. I love adding the okra at the last minute to keep that crunchiness that comes only from fresh okra!

In a medium skillet, heat the oil over medium heat. Once the oil is nice and hot, add the onion and cook, stirring occasionally, for 3 minutes, or until the onion becomes translucent. Add the red pepper flakes, garlic, and shrimp.

Cook for 3 to 4 minutes, or until the shrimp turns pink, then stir in the thyme and basil. Add the okra and cook for an additional 3 minutes, or until the okra begins to brown. Remove the pan from the heat and add salt and pepper to taste. Serve hot.

FIRE-ROASTED OYSTERS WITH RED PEPPER BUTTER

Serves 6

2 red bell peppers, seeded and sliced	½ tablespoon chopped fresh basil	3 dozen oysters, cleaned and scrubbed
¾ cup (165 g) butter, at room temperature	½ teaspoon salt	under cold water
1 tablespoon minced fresh parsley	¼ teaspoon freshly ground black pepper	

Oyster tables can be found in backyards overlooking the salt marshes of the coastal South as well as nearby, in old farm sheds with tractor parts and greasy wrenches lying around. While you might be picturing this as a summertime treat, oyster roasts actually start around the holidays and run only through late February.

Much like the pig pickin', oyster roasts are about family traditions and being around the people you love, sharing the same stories and jokes year after year around a huge table of food. My family always celebrates the day after Christmas with a huge family oyster roast. There are some faces that aren't with us anymore, but we still celebrate on the same old table in my father's shop every year. When I was younger, it didn't seem like a big deal, but now that I am older with kids of my own, it's one of my favorite food traditions.

There are plenty of ways to roast oysters, from gas grills to steamer pots—even a sheet of metal over an open fire. However, I recommend cooking them as in the recipe that follows so that the oysters pick up some of the smoke. It's an enjoyable layer of flavor.

In a food processor, combine the bell peppers, butter, parsley, basil, salt, and black pepper. Process until well combined and set aside.

Prepare a charcoal grill for smoking (see page 25). When the grill is ready, place the oysters on the grill grate with the cup sides facing down. Grill over direct heat for 2 to 4 minutes, or just until the oysters open. Set the oysters aside until cool enough to handle.

With an oyster knife, slowly open an oyster. With a paring knife, cut the back of the oyster to separate it from the shell. Place the oyster back in the shell and put ½ teaspoon of the red pepper butter on the oyster. Repeat for all the oysters, then return them to the grill and cook for a minute, or until the butter is melted and hot. Serve immediately.

FROGMORE STEW, A.K.A. THE LOW COUNTRY BOIL

Serves 10 to 12

2 lemons, quartered

4 bay leaves

5 tablespoons (90 g) salt

3 tablespoons (18 g) freshly ground
   black pepper

4 cloves garlic

1 cup (115 g) Old Bay seasoning, divided

4 pounds (1.8 kg) red potatoes, quartered

2 pounds (905 g) smoked sausage,
   cut into 2-inch (5 cm) pieces

1 large sweet onion, sliced

8 ears corn, cut in half

4 pounds (1.8 kg) large shrimp, unpeeled

Frogmore Stew is a staple of the Low Country, yet the origins of the dish are something of a mystery. One theory about the dish is that local shrimpers in the Frogmore area created a filling meal using what they had readily available from their catch of the day. Another story that specially references the name "Frogmore Stew" can be attributed to Richard Gay, who claims he made this dish in Beaufort for his shipmates when he was stationed there with the National Guard in the 1960s. Gay then carried the recipe back to his home in Frogmore and offered it at his local market as a package deal, with all of the ingredients. No matter the true story behind the dish, it has become a summertime favorite. You'll find it's best enjoyed outside on a huge table lined with newspaper, surrounded by family and friends.

Fill a large stockpot with 6 quarts (5.7 l) of water. Add the lemons, bay leaves, salt, black pepper, garlic, and ½ cup (58 g) of the Old Bay. Cover the pot and bring to a boil over high heat.

Add the potatoes and cook for 6 minutes. Add the smoked sausage and onion and cook for 6 minutes. Add the corn and cook until it is just cooked, about 5 minutes. At this point, the potatoes should also be tender. If not, you can remove the corn to let the potatoes finish cooking.

Turn the heat off, add the corn back in, if it was removed, and add the shrimp. Stir gently for 3 minutes, or until the shrimp are pink and tender. Drain the contents in a large colander or basket (you may need a hand for this!).

Pour everything out on a table lined with newspaper. Remove and discard the bay leaves. Sprinkle the remaining ½ cup Old Bay over the top. Dig in!

OKRA STEW

Serves 10 to 12

5 slices bacon, diced

1 large onion, diced

1 tablespoon minced garlic

⅓ cup (80 ml) Worcestershire sauce

½ tablespoon chopped fresh oregano

1 tablespoon chopped fresh thyme

1 tablespoon freshly ground black pepper

1½ cups (355 ml) chicken stock

5 cups (1.1 kg) crushed tomatoes

4 cups (1.1 kg) diced okra

Okra Stew is a classic Gullah dish that has been on the tables of people in the Low Country since the 1700s. The first documented recipe for Okra Stew can be found in Mary Randolph's book The Virginia Housewife, *published in 1824. Long before it appeared in the Low Country, its direct origins can be traced back to West Africa. Up and down the coast of Africa a version of this soup was eaten, often cooked with rice and vegetables, and sometimes meat. The soup is fairly simplistic, but it is packed full of rich flavors. It's a great weeknight meal when the weather begins to cool off.*

In a large stockpot, place the bacon over medium heat. When the bacon begins to brown, about 5 minutes, add the onion. Cook, stirring occasionally, until the onion is transparent, about 3 minutes.

Add the garlic and cook, stirring, just until fragrant. Add the Worcestershire sauce, oregano, thyme, pepper, and chicken stock. Reduce the heat to medium-low and add the crushed tomatoes. Cook for 25 minutes, stirring about every 5 minutes.

Add the okra and cook for an additional 5 minutes. Serve hot with a side of cornbread.

Note: Make sure you wait to put the okra in! If it's placed in the soup any earlier than directed, it will become mushy.

(continued)

THE
GULLAH PEOPLE

If you aren't familiar with the Low Country of South Carolina and Georgia, you may not understand who the Gullah people are and their cultural significance to the region. The origin of the word *Gullah* isn't clear. Some historical scholars suggest that it is a derivative of the word *Angola*, which is where some of the ancestors of the region came from. The Gullahs also are known as Geechee, which derives from the Ogeechee River just outside Savannah, Georgia. Finally, some believe the word *Gullah* comes from the word originally used to describe the Creole dialect used by the people in this region. The Creole language that the Gullah people spoke was long viewed as a sign of poor English. In 1929 Lorenzo Dow Turner, a professor at South Carolina State University, began hearing students speak in this distinct dialect. As he researched, he began to realize it was not poor language; it simply was the blending of words from the dialects of African tribes from which the speakers' ancestors had come. In 1949 he published *Africanisms in the Gullah Dialect*, which cited more than 3,800 words that were derived from 31 different African countries.

While a majority of the Gullah people came from what is known as the Rice Coast in the Sierra Leone region of Africa, there were also many other people who were brought to this region from other parts of Africa, such as the Gold Coast, the Congo, and Angola. As the rice boom began in the Low Country, the Gullah people settled in the small barrier islands along the coast, which were very close to the rice plantations and very often far away from the plantation owners. Because of this remoteness, the Gullah people were able to preserve traditions from their home country. Although the Gullah people came from different tribes with different traditions, these traditions all were widely accepted and eventually became the traditions of the Gullah people. Their diet remained largely the same as they continued to eat things like okra and rice that they had consumed in their own countries. Naturally, because of their surroundings, coastal fish and shrimp became an important part of their diet. Through all of the struggles that the Gullah people have faced, they still can be found on the coastal barrier islands just as they have been for centuries.

BRUNSWICK "GEORGIA" STEW *(pictured on page 111)*

Serves 8

½ cup (1 stick, 112 g) butter

1 large onion, diced

2 cloves garlic, minced

3 tablespoons (45 ml)
  Worcestershire sauce

2 cups (500 g) Memphis-Style BBQ Sauce
  (page 126)

½ cup (120 ml) apple cider vinegar

¼ teaspoon cayenne pepper

2 cans (14½ ounces [411 g] each)
  diced tomatoes

1½ cups (240 g) lima beans

1½ cups (225 g) corn

2 cups (475 ml) chicken broth

1 pound (455 g) smoked pork
  (leftovers are perfect)

1 pound (455 g) cooked chicken,
  shredded (again, leftovers are great)

2 to 3 cups (400 to 600 g) diced potatoes,
  blanched

1 tablespoon (18 g) salt

½ teaspoon freshly ground black pepper

Is Brunswick Stew from Georgia or Virginia? That question has bounced around the South for a long time. The debate centers around two areas: Brunswick County, Virginia, and Brunswick, Georgia. Virginians claim the dish originated in their county in 1828: While state legislators were on a hunting expedition, their head chef invented the hardy dish for the hungry and cold men. However, in 1898, a 25-gallon (95 l) pot and plaque declaring it the original cooking vessel of "Brunswick Stew" was erected in St. Simons Island, Georgia. This is a debate that will never truly be settled, but I do think everyone would probably agree that the American Indians were probably cooking a form of this stew well before American settlers did!

The two stews are similar in that both have a base of tomatoes and vegetables. The main difference is the meat. The Virginia stew uses mainly chicken, though early recipes also have some squirrel and venison. The Georgia version uses beef and pork instead. Everyone has their own variations and ways they cook Brunswick Stew as well. What all these stews have in common is that they are not a fast and easy thing. This is a recipe that takes time to cook. Luckily, it also has a nice payoff as there aren't many things as rewarding as a pot of Brunswick Stew on a cool fall evening. This recipe uses smoked pork and chicken, but if you have leftover brisket, by all means throw it in the pot as well.

(continued)

In a Dutch oven, heat the butter over medium heat. When the butter melts and becomes foamy, about 3 minutes, add the onion and garlic. Sauté until soft, about 4 minutes. Add the Worcestershire sauce, BBQ sauce, vinegar, and cayenne. Stir until the mixture is well combined and let cook for 2 minutes, or just until it begins to bubble.

Add the tomatoes, lima beans, corn, and chicken broth. Stir to combine. Add the smoked pork and chicken, then stir to combine. Reduce the heat to medium-low and cook for an hour, stirring periodically to prevent burning. Add the potatoes, salt, and black pepper and cook for an additional 20 minutes. Serve hot with a side of cornbread.

Brunswick "Georgia" Stew (page 109) ▶

FUNERAL GRITS

Serves 6 to 8

2 cups (475 ml) whole milk

2 cups (475 ml) heavy cream

1 cup (148 g) stone-ground or
  coarse-ground grits

3 tablespoons (42 g) butter

2 cups (225 g) shredded Cheddar cheese

¼ teaspoon cayenne pepper

1 tablespoon paprika

Salt to taste

Freshly ground black pepper to taste

4 eggs, beaten

1 large green bell pepper, diced

2 green onions, sliced

When someone has a family member pass in the South, the first thing that pops into most people's minds is "We have to carry the family food." Generally, this means you need to get a casserole cooking. Funeral Grits work as a side dish that can be cooked ahead and held at a low temperature for long periods of time. Because many people also enjoy grits for breakfast, they do double duty reheated the next morning for a quick bite. The creaminess of the grits and cheese combined with the crunch of bell pepper is the ultimate bit of comfort.

Grease a 9 × 9-inch (23 × 23 cm) baking dish and set aside.

Preheat the oven to 350°F (180°C). In a heavy-bottomed saucepan over medium heat, bring the milk and heavy cream to a slow boil. Using a wooden spoon, gradually stir in the grits, stirring constantly (see note).

Reduce the heat to a low simmer and continue to cook for 20 minutes, stirring occasionally.

Add the butter and stir until it is completely melted. Then add the Cheddar, cayenne, paprika, and salt and black pepper to taste. Stir until well combined. Add the eggs, bell pepper, and green onions and cook for 3 to 5 minutes, or until thick.

Slowly spoon the mixture into the baking dish. Bake for 45 minutes, or until golden brown. Serve this dish warm as a side.

Note: You really do have to stir grits constantly! Make sure you are scraping the bottom of the pot to keep the grits from burning. Try to keep the sides of your pot clean, as grits that stay on the side of the pot will cook, harden, and no doubt eventually end up falling into the pot.

HOPPIN' JOHN

Serves 6

2 tablespoons (28 g) butter

6 ounces (170 g) country ham, finely diced

1 cup (120 g) finely diced celery

1 small onion, diced

1 bell pepper, diced

2 cloves garlic, minced

6 cups (1.4 l) chicken stock

4 cups (660 g) cooked black-eyed peas
  (canned is okay)

2 bay leaves

1½ teaspoons salt

1 teaspoon dried thyme

½ teaspoon freshly ground black pepper

1½ cups (293 g) uncooked rice

2 pounds (905 g) okra, sliced

Green onions, for garnish

Hoppin' John has always been viewed as a New Year's Day dish in the South. The origin of the dish falls into the category of Southern food that was based on traditions in West Africa and brought by slaves who yearned for the flavor of home. Over time, it was adapted to use what was readily available at the local grocery store. The first time it appeared in a cookbook was in 1847, with Sarah Rutledge's Carolina Housewife. *As for the name, she did not provide a definitive answer, and there are many stories out there. My favorite is that the name comes from an old crippled man who hocked peas and rice around the city markets of downtown Charleston, whose name was John.*

Most recipes these days use black-eyed peas, but traditional recipes call for the use of cow peas or red peas. If you want to go all in, do yourself a favor and order Carolina Gold rice and Sea Island red peas from Anson Mills and taste the history of this dish. Take your time and let the flavors marry together.

In a heavy-bottomed pot, such as a Dutch oven, heat the butter and ham over medium heat. Once the butter has melted, add the celery, onion, and bell pepper and cook for 3 to 4 minutes, or until the onion begins to soften. Add the garlic and cook, stirring constantly, for 1 minute.

Add the chicken stock, black-eyed peas, and bay leaves. Cook for 8 minutes, stirring occasionally. Add the salt, thyme, black pepper, and rice. Reduce the heat to medium-low and cook for 15 minutes, stirring occasionally. When the rice is close to finished, add the okra and cook for 3 minutes. Remove and discard the bay leaves.

Serve hot with green onions as a garnish, and hopefully a slice of cornbread.

RED RICE

Serves 10 to 12

2 cups (390 g) uncooked white rice	1½ tablespoons (15 g) minced garlic	1 can (28 ounces, 800 g)
1 quart (946 ml) water	½ lemon	crushed tomatoes
14 ounces (395 g) smoked sausage,	⅓ cup (85 g) Memphis-Style BBQ Sauce	2 tablespoons (36 g) sea salt
cut into ¼-inch (0.5 cm) slices	(page 126)	1 teaspoon freshly ground black pepper
1 medium white onion, diced	⅓ cup (80 ml) Worcestershire sauce	1 tablespoon garlic salt
2 tablespoons (28 g) salted butter	½ cup (50 g) sliced green onions	

For 300 years, Red Rice has been a staple on tables across the Low Country. You will see rice as a main ingredient across the region because at one point in history, the coast of North and South Carolina was the most prosperous rice-growing area in the world. Early recipes for Red Rice would specify that only long-grain rice such as Carolina Gold, an heirloom breed, could be used.

Like many dishes in this area, Red Rice can be traced back to Gullah cuisine. It has become one of the most recognizable and culturally important dishes that have ever come out of the Low Country. Every time I cook red rice, I think of how a dish now enjoyed by millions of people came from the darkest time in our region's history. The next time you are sitting in a fine dining restaurant in Charleston, or Savannah, or even on the tailgate of your truck at a small barbecue joint in Garland, North Carolina, eating Red Rice, realize you are eating history.

Start by cooking your rice in the oven. Preheat the oven to 350°F (180°C). In a large casserole dish, combine the rice, water, and a pinch of salt. With your hands, mix the water and rice until the water becomes cloudy—you are essentially washing it.

Cover the casserole dish with foil, making sure the foil is on as tight as you can get it. Bake for 20 to 30 minutes. Keep an eye on it: If your rice begins to look dry, add ⅓ cup (80 ml) of water. Start tasting around 20 minutes; when the rice is tender, remove the dish from the oven and set aside.

(continued)

While the rice is cooking, in a large pot over medium heat, combine the smoked sausage, onion, and butter. Cook, stirring occasionally, until the onion is translucent, about 5 minutes.

Add the garlic and stir for about 30 seconds, then add a squeeze of lemon juice to prevent the garlic from burning. Add the tomatoes, sea salt, pepper, and garlic salt. Stir well until the spices are thoroughly combined. Reduce the heat to medium-low and cook for 20 minutes, stirring occasionally.

Slowly pour the tomato mixture over top of the cooked rice. Mix the rice and tomatoes until they are well combined.

Return the casserole dish to the oven and bake for 10 minutes. Serve hot.

RICE PLANTATIONS
IN THE LOW COUNTRY

The efforts of the first early planters of rice in the Low Country proved to be futile; they learned very quickly that growing such a specialized crop there without any expertise was extremely hard. The planters soon realized that they would have to rely on African slaves from areas such as Sierra Leone who could bring their methods of growing rice from their home countries. By the early 18th century, rice had become a major cash crop for the Low Country region. Aiding in the growth of rice as a huge cash crop was the fact that ports like Charleston were easily accessible to ships traveling up and down the Atlantic seaboard. Rice continued to be a huge cash crop until after the Civil War. But as labor became scarce and the planters dealt with the threat of hurricanes coming through year after year and destroying levees and rice patties, the once prosperous rice industry dwindled, and by the early 1900s, growers of rice had disappeared. That is, until an inquisitive California boy, by way of the University of North Carolina at Chapel Hill, became extremely curious about food history and, in particular, the food history of the Low Country. When he tried to re-create dishes for celebratory dinners offering era-authentic menus, he quickly realized that many of the ingredients no longer existed and that South Carolina farmers had no interest in growing antebellum grains such as Carolina Gold rice.

Over the next several years he researched and grew small plots of Carolina Gold rice and made it his life mission to bring the rice and other long-forgotten grains back to life. In 2000, he produced his first real crop of Carolina Gold rice, along with 10 varieties of heirloom corn. As word grew throughout the chef community, the popularity of his company grew quickly. The name of that California boy who fell in love with the Low Country is Glenn Roberts, and he owns Anson Mills. As someone who loves the history of the food I cook, I am extremely grateful for farmers like him who have made it their life's mission to provide people like me with a product that is part of our past—even something as small as a grain of rice.

LIKKER PUDDING

Serves 6

3 medium sweet potatoes

3 eggs, beaten

1½ cups (300 g) sugar

1½ cups (125 g) shredded dried coconut, divided

2 teaspoons ground cinnamon

1 tablespoon (15 ml) vanilla extract

5 tablespoons (15 ml) dark rum

I have seen this dish referred to as Caribbean-Style Sweet Potatoes, but after I saw it called Likker Pudding in a 1950s cookbook, I adopted the name. With the coconut, cinnamon, and rum, it's a dish that really shows the influence of the West Indies in the cooking of the Low Country. I recommend using dark rum for a bolder flavor that better accentuates the coconut. It pairs well alongside turkey or chicken.

Grease a 9 × 9-inch (23 × 23 cm) baking dish. Preheat the oven to 350°F (180°C). Bake the sweet potatoes for 45 minutes, or until they are tender.

Remove the sweet potatoes from the oven and set them aside until they are cool enough to handle. Leave the oven on, though. With a large spoon, scoop the inside of the potatoes out into a large mixing bowl. You can discard the skins.

Add the eggs, sugar, 1 cup (85 g) of the coconut, the cinnamon, vanilla, and rum. Mix until well combined, then pour into the casserole dish. Bake for 45 minutes, or until the pudding has set. Remove the dish from the oven and let it start to cool.

On a baking sheet, toast the remaining ½ cup (40 g) coconut for about 3 minutes. Garnish the sweet potatoes with the toasted coconut and serve warm.

MEMPHIS AND THE DELTA

Ribs, Catfish, and Tamales

My first plate of barbecue in Memphis didn't come from one of the famous joints like the Charlie Vergos Rendezvous, Interstate Barbecue, or Central BBQ. No, I was eating at an unassuming place in west Memphis called Ray's Bar-B-Que. I still remember that plate, though, loaded down with fried catfish, Memphis slaw, baked beans, and, of course, dry-rub ribs. I was fascinated with the flavor of the ribs, how the spices mixed with the hickory smoke—I even liked the side of sweet sauce. Little did I know, that plate of food would shape the way I cook nearly 20 years later.

I still make frequent trips to this region of the South, and this chapter is my best effort at a "greatest hits" of sorts. In addition to the dishes you'd expect to find, like those ribs and fried catfish, you'll likely be surprised by a few recipes I consider signatures of the region. For example, look no further than the Delta Tamales (see page 129). While tamales are a Mexican specialty, they've also become commonplace throughout the Delta—with a few regional changes, of course. I think you'll find they're every bit as good as the ribs!

MEMPHIS DRY-RUB RIBS

Serves 4 to 6

For the Memphis Dry Rub

1 cup (112 g) paprika

6 tablespoons (36 g) freshly ground
   black pepper

4 tablespoons (28 g) onion powder

¼ cup (26 g) celery seed

2 cups (450 g) packed brown sugar

6 tablespoons (18 g) dried oregano

2 tablespoons dried thyme

4 tablespoons (36 g) mustard powder

6 tablespoons (108 g) salt

½ cup (60 g) chili powder

For the Mop

1 cup (235 ml) vinegar

1 cup (235 ml) water

½ cup (70 g) Memphis Dry Rub

2 racks baby back ribs, about 1½ pounds
   (680 g) each

Memphis-Style BBQ Sauce (page 126),
   for serving

In my restaurant, I've adopted Memphis-style ribs. Their signature flavor comes from a unique rub, featuring ingredients like oregano, celery seed, and onion powder. Since Memphis was a major city on the Mississippi River trade route from New Orleans, residents had access to spices like these that were unavailable in other parts of the South. The recipe that follows draws on these flavors and is my homage to Memphis-style ribs. Besides cooking low and slow, my only advice is to cook these on a Saturday night surrounded by friends, with B.B. King playing in the background.

To make the dry rub: In a bowl or an airtight storage container, mix all rub ingredients together with a fork, making sure they are well combined. This rub can be held for up to 3 months when sealed.

To make the mop: In a mixing bowl, combine the vinegar, water, and rub and whisk together. Set aside.

Prepare a grill for smoking (see page 25). To prepare the ribs, flip them over so that the bone side is facing up. Slide the tip of a dull knife under the membrane covering the back of the ribs. Lift and loosen the membrane until it breaks loose, then grab the corner of the membrane and pull it completely off. This will help create an even smoke ring on your ribs.

Season the ribs with about ½ cup (70 g) of the rub, making sure the ribs are coated. Massage the rub into the ribs to make sure it sticks. Place the ribs bone side down on the grill and cook, covered, for 1 hour.

Take the lid off your grill and brush the ribs with the mop sauce. Place the lid back on, cook for 30 minutes, and baste again. Cook for a final 30 minutes, or until the ribs are tender and the bones become exposed.

To serve, cut each rack in three-bone sections and sprinkle about ½ cup (70 g) (or more, if desired) of the remaining rub over the top. (Save and store the rest of the rub for the next time you make ribs.) Serve with a side of Memphis-Style BBQ Sauce.

(sauce recipe follows)

MEMPHIS-STYLE BBQ SAUCE

Makes 3 cups (750 g)

2 cups (480 g) ketchup

½ cup (115 g) packed brown sugar

1 tablespoon onion powder

1 teaspoon salt

2 teaspoons garlic salt

½ cup (88 g) mustard

1 tablespoon freshly ground black pepper

2 tablespoons (30 ml)
Worcestershire sauce

1 cup (322 g) pancake syrup
(not maple syrup; you want the
high sugar content of the syrup)

1 tablespoon (15 ml) hot sauce

In a 3-quart (2.8 l) pot, combine all ingredients and whisk together until well mixed. Over medium heat, bring to a low boil. Reduce the heat to low and cook, stirring occasionally, for 20 minutes.

Remove from the heat and let cool. Store in an airtight container in the refrigerator until ready to serve. It can be held for up to a week.

MEMPHIS-STYLE SLAW

Serves 8

For the Dressing

¼ cup (44 g) yellow mustard

¼ cup (60 ml) apple cider vinegar

1 cup (200 g) sugar

½ cup (115 g) packed brown sugar

Salt to taste

Freshly ground black pepper to taste

For the Slaw

1 pound (455 g) shredded cabbage
   or coleslaw mix

½ green bell pepper, finely diced

2 tablespoons celery seed

Dash of hot sauce, such as Crystal

Being an Eastern North Carolina boy, I must admit I have always preferred our sweet slaw! Yet I have grown to enjoy the tangy, mustard-based slaw that they serve at legendary rib joints like Charlie Vergos Rendezvous. My advice when riffing on these slaw recipes is to skip the fancy mustard and just go for regular yellow mustard instead. It's the key to the right flavor. The crunchiness of the bell pepper adds a fresh pop to this slaw as well, so don't leave it out. Serve with ribs or try with some of your other favorite barbecue dishes.

To make the dressing: In a small bowl, combine the mustard, vinegar, and sugars. Whisk until the sugars have dissolved, then add salt and black pepper to taste.

To make the slaw: In a large bowl, combine the cabbage or coleslaw mix, bell pepper, and celery seed. Pour the dressing over the slaw mixture and gently toss the salad until well combined. Add a shake or two of hot sauce and toss the salad one more time. Refrigerate for 30 minutes before serving.

DELTA TAMALES

Makes about 30 tamales

For the Pork Filling

⅓ cup (80 ml) vegetable oil

1 medium onion, diced

6 pounds (2.7 kg) pork shoulder,
 cut up into 1½-inch (3½ cm) chunks

3 tablespoons (54 g) salt

¼ cup (30 g) chili powder

3 tablespoons (21 g) paprika

2 tablespoons freshly ground black pepper

1 teaspoon cayenne

1 teaspoon red pepper flakes

1 tablespoon garlic powder

2 packages (8 ounces [225 g] each)
 dried corn husks

For the Tamale Dough

3½ cups (448 g) masa harina

1½ cups (300 g) lard

3 cups (710 ml) hot water

2 tablespoons (36 g) salt

1 tablespoon ground cumin

The Delta tamale is a bit different from a traditional Mexican tamale, as it is a little smaller and the dough is made of cornmeal rather than masa. They are also simmered in a spicy broth rather than being steamed in the corn husk. This recipe is my take on the Delta tamale, with one step closer to Mexico. It is made like a traditional Mexican tamale, with masa, and cooked in a corn husk. However, after the tamales are finished, I open them up and pour spicy broth on them.

To make the pork filling: In a 16-quart (15 l) stockpot, heat the oil over medium-high heat. Once the oil begins to shimmer, add the onion and pork. Cook for 3 to 4 minutes, or until the pork browns, then add the salt. Stir and add enough water to the pot to cover the pork and onion. Reduce the heat to medium-low and simmer, covered, until the meat is tender, about 2 to 2½ hours.

Take the pot off the heat and remove the pork from the cooking liquid and set aside. Once the pork is cool enough to handle, remove and discard any skin and big chunks of fat. Shred or dice the meat and return it to the pot. Turn the burner back on to medium. Add the chili powder, paprika, black pepper, cayenne, red pepper flakes, and garlic powder. Cook, stirring occasionally, for 10 minutes. Set aside.

To prepare the corn husks: While the meat mixture is cooking, soak the husks in a large bowl or a small sink filled with hot water. They can soak until you're ready to use them, but make sure to soak for at least 45 minutes so that they are soft and pliable. When you are ready to use them, remove them from the water and gently dry them off with a paper towel.

(continued)

To make the dough: In a large mixing bowl, combine all of the dough ingredients. Mix the dough by hand until it is well combined. The dough should be moist but not wet; it should look like soft cake batter. Cover the mixture with a warm, moist towel until you are ready to use it, no more than 3 hours.

Note: A trick to making sure you have fluffy dough is to drop a small piece of dough into a cup of cold water. If it floats, it's ready. If it doesn't float, mix the dough a little more and add some additional lard.

To assemble and cook the tamales: After removing the corn husks from the water and drying them, cut or rip them into ¼-inch (0.5 cm) pieces that are about 8 to 10 inches (20 to 25 cm) long.

One at a time, lay each corn husk flat with the pointy end facing you. Spread about ¼ cup of the dough out on the corn husk until it makes a 4-inch (10 cm) circle. Spoon about 1½ teaspoons of the meat mixture down the middle of the tamale.

Take both long sides of the tamale and bring them together. You'll know you did this right if the batter completely surrounds the filling. Tuck one side under the other and roll. Take the bottom part of the husk and fold it under. Tie the flap with corn husk strips or string; do not tie them too tight, though, as the tamales need room to expand.

Place the tamales in a steamer basket with the folded bottoms pointing down. Place the leftover corn husks over the top of the tamales. Steam the tamales over medium heat, making sure that the water does not touch them and that it doesn't boil away. When the tamales are finished, the corn husks should easily peel away from the masa.

To serve, open up the wrappers and pour the reheated cooking liquid over the top.

THE ORIGINS OF
DELTA
TAMALES

"Hot tamales and they're hot, she got 'em for sale. She got two for a nickel and four for a dime."

Those are the lyrics from the song "They're Red Hot" by Robert Johnson, recorded in 1935. Why in the world would a legendary blues singer in the Delta be singing about the "Tamale Lady"? Well, there are a couple of theories about how the tamale became commonplace in the Delta.

One theory is that after Mississippi soldiers fought in the Spanish-American War, they came home and missed the new flavors they had tasted. Scribbled recipes in journals led to the cornmeal version of the tamale. The other theory is that like many other food traditions in the South, tamales were brought here with the migrant workers who arrived to work on farms. The tamales were a taste of home. (This could well be the case because in the early 20th century, the boom of cotton plantations brought many workers in from Mexico.)

No matter how the tamale arrived, locals soon saw the appeal. In addition to the addictive flavors, tamales are practical. Wrapped in corn husks, they stay warm and moist, making them much different from, say, a leftover biscuit. The lore of the tamale began to grow in communities, with street vendors popping up on corners hocking "Fresh Hot Tamales," no different from street vendors in Mexico City selling them today.

DUCK AND OYSTER GUMBO *(pictured on page 135)*

Serves 12

6 boneless duck breasts or 6 boneless,
   skinless, fresh local chicken breasts
   (about 8 ounces [225 g] each)

Salt to taste

Freshly ground black pepper to taste

6 tablespoons (85 g) salted butter, divided

8 ounces (225 g) thick-cut bacon, sliced

1 pound (455 g) andouille sausage,
   cut into ¼-inch (0.5 cm) slices

¼ cup (60 ml) vegetable oil

½ cup (63 g) flour

1 large onion, diced

1 bell pepper, diced

2 ribs celery, diced

8 cloves garlic, finely minced

4 cups (950 ml) chicken broth

2 cups (475 ml) hot water

½ cup (120 ml) Worcestershire sauce

1 can (28 ounces, 800 g)
   crushed tomatoes

3 pounds (1.4 kg) okra, cut into
   ½-inch (1 cm) pieces

1 pint (473 ml) oysters, drained

6 cups (990 g) cooked rice, for serving

Sliced green onions, for garnish

Fried Skillet Cornbread (page 168),
   for serving

While gumbo is a dish that will always be associated with the melting pot of cultures that is New Orleans, it combines ingredients and culinary practices of several cultures, including French, Spanish, German, Filipino, West African, and Choctaw. Here, I use it to highlight fresh duck and local rice, but I keep the rest of the recipe fairly traditional. The wait for a great pot of gumbo is so worth it; it truly can warm your soul on a dreary winter night.

Slice the duck breasts into ½-inch (1 cm) strips and season with salt and black pepper to taste. In a Dutch oven over medium-high heat, melt 1 tablespoon (14 g) of the butter. Add the duck strips. When you begin to hear the duck sizzle, similar to the sizzle of bacon, cook for about 4 minutes. Flip the duck and cook for an additional 4 minutes. Remove from the pot and set aside.

Reduce the heat to medium and add the bacon. Cook until browned through and sizzling. Remove the bacon from the pot and set it aside. At this point, the bottom of your pot should be looking a little dirty—resist the urge to clean it! Just keep cooking. Add the andouille sausage and cook until browned, stirring constantly. (The crisper you get the sausage, the hotter it will get.) Remove the sausage and set aside.

(continued)

The next step is key: making the roux. Reduce the heat to low and add the vegetable oil. Use a whisk to loosen up all the particles stuck on the bottom of the pot. Slowly add the flour, whisking constantly. Once the flour is incorporated, add 2 tablespoons (28 g) of the butter. Increase the heat to medium-low and continue to whisk for 10 minutes (see note). Your roux should have a pastelike consistency at this point. If it doesn't, add some additional butter. Or, if it appears to be too runny, add an additional tablespoon of flour. The roux will go from a light khaki color to dark brown as it cooks. Once the roux becomes dark brown, remove the pot from the heat and let it cool.

While the roux is cooling, dice the bacon into small pieces. You can also cut the duck into smaller pieces if you'd like. Return the Dutch oven with the roux to the stovetop and place over medium heat. Add the onion, bell pepper, and celery (also known as the Holy Trinity) along with the remaining butter and the garlic. Cook, stirring occasionally, until the onion becomes translucent, about 5 minutes. Add the chicken broth, water, and Worcestershire sauce. Stir in the tomatoes, duck, sausage, and bacon and bring to a simmer. Cook, covered, for 30 minutes. I recommend removing the lid to stir the mixture about every 5 minutes or so.

Add the okra and cook for 10 minutes. (I normally don't recommend cooking okra very long, but with gumbo it's different and the okra's juices will help make your gumbo thicker.) About 3 to 5 minutes before you are ready to serve the gumbo, add the oysters. Serve the gumbo in bowls over white rice, garnished with green onions and a side of cornbread.

Note: Gumbo can seem intimidating to most home cooks because gumbo recipes include a long list of ingredients and an even longer list of instructions, but it isn't that complex. It just takes time. The hardest part is the roux, and my best advice is to take your time and work slowly. If you want to take longer than 10 minutes to stir your roux, that's fine. Work at your pace until you get the hang of it.

Duck and Oyster Gumbo (page 133) ▶

COUNTRY-STYLE DUCK WITH ONION GRAVY

Serves 4

2 cups (250 g) flour, divided

8 small duck breasts (such as teal) or
   4 regular-sized duck breasts, cut in half

½ cup (120 ml) canola oil

2 tablespoons (28 g) butter, divided

1 large white onion, sliced thin

1 teaspoon salt

½ teaspoon freshly ground black pepper

¼ teaspoon chopped fresh thyme

4 cups (950 ml) chicken broth, divided

Cooked rice, for serving

The Delta is defined by water: Nearly 40 percent of North America's water flows through this region. It is full of rivers, swamps, and flooded rice fields. It also has numerous waterfowl preserves, making it home to some of the finest duck hunting in the world. You may have the energy for something more ambitious the day after a duck hunt, like the gumbo on page 133. However, when I get home from walking through Mississippi mud, I want something easy and hearty. This simple dish is all about the star ingredients, which are Delta staples.

In a pan or on a baking sheet, pour 1¼ cups (155 g) of the flour. Season the duck breasts with salt and pepper to taste on each side, then place the duck breasts in the flour. With your hands, press the flour into the duck breasts on each side until they are coated with the flour.

In a Dutch oven, heat the oil over medium heat. When the oil begins to shimmer, place the duck in the oil. Cook for 5 minutes on each side. Remove the duck breasts from the pan and set aside.

Add 1 tablespoon of the butter to the pan and let it melt, then add the onion. Cook for about 6 minutes, or until it becomes tender, stirring to prevent burning. Add the remaining 1 tablespoon butter and reduce the heat to medium-low. Slowly add the remaining ¾ cup (95 g) flour, whisking to combine. Continue to whisk for 3 to 5 minutes, or until the mixture begins to brown.

Add the salt, pepper, thyme, and 2 cups (475 ml) of the chicken broth. Stir the mixture until it begins to thicken. Add the duck breasts and the remaining 2 cups (475 ml) chicken broth, and stir a few more times. Cook, covered, for 25 to 30 minutes, stirring occasionally. Serve hot with rice and spoon the extra gravy over the top.

DUCK HUNTING

When I was a teenager, I read the stories of Nash Buckingham, which described hunting on the swamps and bayous of places like Beaver Dam and talked about hunting blinds like the "Hand Worker Blind." Ever since, I have been mesmerized with the mystique of hunting in the Delta. But what makes this area so special and unique? What makes a young boy lie in bed at night and dream of sitting in 20°F (-7°C) weather as the sun comes up? What makes an old man slough 250 yards through a rice field at 6 in the morning? The answer to all of these questions is very simple: ducks.

Why are there so many ducks in the Delta? The Delta is situated in the middle of the Mississippi Flyway, which is named after not the state but the river. It is one of the four major flyways that migratory birds travel on as they fly from their summer breeding grounds in Canada to their wintering sites in the southern United States, Mexico, and South America. Birds travel the Mackenzie, Missouri, Mississippi, and Ohio rivers south until the concentration is focused mainly on the lower Mississippi River Valley; a picture of their migratory pattern would resemble a funnel. In the middle of that funnel is the Delta and Arkansas. The region's natural habitat of plentiful bayous and swamps, along with the benefits of agriculture, makes it the perfect spot for duck hunting. It is estimated that 40 percent of all waterfowl in North America travel along this route every year, just as they have for centuries.

I have been extremely lucky through the years to spend time hunting in places like Beaver Dam and the hole where the Hand Worker Blind was in that I read about so many years ago. If you are a waterfowler, taking a trip to the Mississippi Flyway is something you will never forget; it's a magical place that will call to you after you leave. When you feel that first cool north wind of fall, your mind will take you back there. After 25 years of spending time there, I still miss it immediately when I get on a plane to head home.

GRILLED PORK TENDERLOIN WITH TOMATO AND GREENS RAGU *(pictured on page 141)*

Serves 4

Ragu

4 teaspoons (20 ml) olive oil

1 medium onion, diced

2 cloves garlic, minced

¼ teaspoon red pepper flakes

5 cups (150 g) greens, such as spinach, escarole, or turnip

2 cans (14½ ounces [411 g] each) diced tomatoes

2 whole pork tenderloins (about 1 pound [455 g] each)

Pork Tenderloin Rub

1 teaspoon garlic salt

1 teaspoon freshly ground black pepper

1 teaspoon dried parsley

½ teaspoon dried oregano

½ teaspoon garlic powder

I've done a lot of cooking in an unassuming house in Sledge, Mississippi. It's not a fancy kitchen. The countertops are often cluttered with duck calls, coffee cups, and the occasional wine glass. The reason I love this kitchen is the people I've shared it with: my father, uncle, cousin, and friends. After a day of hunting, this is the recipe I'll make, served up family-style on a huge platter. The ragu—which gets its sweetness from the tomatoes, aided by the garlic—is a perfect way to use fresh greens to liven up a basic grilled pork tenderloin. When it's poured over the top of the rich pork loin, the ragu creates a perfect balance of sweet and salty heartiness that will warm your soul.

To make the ragu: In a medium saucepan, heat the olive oil over medium heat. Add the onion and cook, stirring often, until softened, about 3 to 5 minutes. Add the garlic and red pepper flakes and stir. Cook for about 1 minute. Stir in the greens and cook for 2 minutes, or until they begin to wilt. Reduce the heat to medium-low and add the tomatoes. Simmer for 10 minutes, then reduce the heat and cover to keep the ragu warm while you grill the pork loins.

(continued)

To make the rub and grill the pork: Prepare a charcoal grill (see page 25). Meanwhile, in a small bowl, combine the rub ingredients and stir with a fork until well mixed. Pat the rub onto the tenderloins and let them sit at room temperature while your grill heats up.

Once the grill is ready, place the tenderloins over direct heat. Cook the tenderloins for 5 to 7 minutes per side, and try to flip them only once. After cooking on both sides, check the internal temperature. From here, the goal is to get the tenderloins in the 140°F to 145°F (60°C to 63°C) range without overcooking them. To do this, move them over indirect heat and continue to cook until they reach the correct internal temperature, about 18 minutes total cooking time. Remove the pork from the grill and let it rest for 10 minutes.

Slice the tenderloins in ¼-inch (0.5 cm) slices and place on a large platter. Spoon the ragu over top and serve immediately.

Grilled Pork Tenderloin with Tomato and Greens Ragu (page 139) ▶

COFFEE-RUBBED BEEF TENDERLOIN

Serves 10 to 12

1 whole beef tenderloin (5 to 6 pounds
   [2.3 to 2.7 kg]), trimmed

2 tablespoons (30 ml) olive oil

1 tablespoon paprika

2 tablespoons (36 g) sea salt

1 teaspoon coarsely ground black pepper

4 teaspoons ground coffee

1 tablespoon sugar

Blue Cheese Horseradish Sauce
   (page 146), optional

When people think of "barbecue," they very seldom think of an elegant dinner. Instead, they usually envision something greasy served outdoors, eaten with your hands, and more than likely ending with a stain on some part of your clothing. This recipe changes that. This is a perfect dish for a family Christmas Eve dinner or a special occasion when you want to woo your guest with your grilling skills. With this recipe you will use your smoker to add a bit of that smoky flavor, but you will finish the beef in the oven to get the perfect doneness. The rub does have a bit of sugar in it to add sweetness to the richness that is developed from the coffee and salt. Slice the tenderloin in ½-inch (1 cm) pieces and serve it hot.

Let the beef sit out at room temperature for 1 hour. Prepare a smoker according to the directions on page 25. Set your smoker to 250°F (120°C).

Pour the olive oil over the top of the tenderloin and use your hands to rub the tenderloin to ensure the olive oil is coating the entire surface. In a small bowl, combine the paprika, sea salt, pepper, coffee, and sugar. Use a fork to mix until well combined. Sprinkle the rub over the tenderloin, pressing the rub in to make sure it sticks.

Place the tenderloin on the smoker. Smoke the tenderloin for 35 to 40 minutes, or until it reaches an internal temperature of 100°F (38°C). Meanwhile, preheat the oven to 400°F (200°C). Remove the tenderloin from the smoker and transfer it to a greased baking sheet. Bake for an additional 25 minutes, or until the thickest part of the tenderloin reaches an internal temperature of 130°F (55°C) for medium-rare. Remove from the oven and let it rest for 15 minutes before slicing. If desired, serve with Blue Cheese Horseradish Sauce.

(sauce recipe follows)

BLUE CHEESE HORSERADISH SAUCE

Makes 2 cups (480 g)

2 tablespoons (28 g) butter

2 cloves garlic, minced

3½ tablespoons (53 g) prepared
horseradish

1½ cups (355 ml) heavy cream

1 teaspoon salt

1½ cups (180 g) crumbled blue cheese

In a saucepan over medium heat, melt the butter. Add the garlic and horseradish and stir for 30 seconds. Add the heavy cream and salt and cook for 3 to 4 minutes, or until the mixture begins to slowly bubble. Add the blue cheese and whisk until the cheese is melted and well combined. When the sauce is smooth, remove it from the heat and serve.

STIR-FRIED COLLARDS WITH SPICY TOMATO CHOW-CHOW

(pictured on page 149)

Serves 6 to 8

For the Chow-Chow

8 large tomatoes, diced

½ cup (75 g) diced hot peppers, such as
  red habaneros or Scotch bonnets

1 large yellow onion, diced

1 cup (200 g) sugar

½ cup (120 ml) white vinegar

1 tablespoon (18 g) sea salt

3 cloves garlic, minced

For the Collards

3 pounds (1.4 kg) collards, cleaned,
  stemmed, and coarsely chopped

1 tablespoon (14 g) butter

1 small red onion, halved and sliced

½ teaspoon sea salt

1 tablespoon (15 ml) sesame oil

5 cloves garlic, diced

1 tablespoon (15 ml) lemon juice

1 tablespoon (15 ml) oyster sauce

½ tablespoon red pepper flakes

1 teaspoon sugar

Plantation owners in the Delta were faced with a labor shortage after the Emancipation Proclamation. Many tried to turn to Chinese immigrants, creating an influx of Chinese into the Delta that soon affected local cuisine. Some of these Chinese became entrepreneurs who left the plantations and opened up small grocery stores in African American neighborhoods—selling to customers who previously bought goods from plantation-owned commissaries. In such a deeply segregated part of the South, the Chinese prospered. Today you won't find as many Chinese-owned businesses in the Delta, but they're still around.

One such business I love is called Chow's Cakes of the Delta, owned by Sally Chow. Their profile in the New York Times *explored how the Chows combine classic Southern ingredients with Chinese cooking techniques. I was hooked and immediately wanted to try my hand at their technique for collards. Rather than cooking collards for a long time, as is traditional, they sear fresh collards in a wok. This is my take on their idea, though I serve it with a side of chow-chow. (Being the Southern boy that I am, I say you can't have collards without chow-chow!) Note that the chow-chow can be made a few days ahead and stored in the refrigerator in an airtight container. That way, when it's time to eat, you can simply fry the collards and serve them up with the chow-chow.*

(continued)

To make the chow-chow: In a 2-quart (1.9 l) pot over medium heat, combine all of the chow-chow ingredients. Stir together until well incorporated. Cook, uncovered, stirring often, for 30 to 45 minutes, or until the mixture becomes thick. Let the chow-chow cool and then place it in an airtight container in the fridge.

To make the collards: Bring a large pot of water to a boil. Add the collards and blanch them for 4 to 5 minutes, giving them a stir from time to time. Be careful not to overcook them; you want to keep that vibrant green color.

Transfer the collards to a colander and run them under cold water until they are cool to the touch. Drain them well and pat dry. Get your wok going over medium heat. Once it's nice and hot, add the butter, let it melt, then add the onion. Cook until the onion begins to really sizzle, about 3 minutes. Increase the heat to high and add the salt and sesame oil. Stir to make sure the wok is completely coated with oil. Add the garlic and cook for 1 minute, or until it becomes aromatic, then add the lemon juice to stop the garlic from burning. Add the collards and cook, stirring constantly, for 1 to 2 minutes. While continuing to stir, add the oyster sauce, red pepper flakes, and sugar. Remove the wok from the heat and serve immediately with chow-chow on the side.

Stir-Fried Collards with Spicy Tomato Chow-Chow (page 147) ▶

MERIGOLD TOMATOES

Serves 6 to 8

2 teaspoons (10 ml) olive oil

1 medium onion, diced

1 bell pepper, diced

½ cup (20 g) chopped fresh basil

2 teaspoons chopped fresh thyme

3 cloves garlic, minced

3 cans (28 ounces [800 g] each)
  diced tomatoes, undrained

1 tablespoon (18 g) salt

1 teaspoon freshly ground black pepper

2½ cups (275 g) Italian bread crumbs

1½ cups (150 g) grated Parmesan cheese

1½ cups (175 g) shredded sharp
  Cheddar cheese

When you're in Mississippi, travel 19 miles (31 km) due south of Alligator, 13 miles (21 km) due north of Cleveland, and just a few miles due east of the legendary blues joint Po' Monkey Lounge. Here, you will find the town of Merigold. Make sure to visit McCarty's Pottery and the Gallery Restaurant, which is the home of a dish that has piqued the interest of many a chef over the years: Merigold Tomatoes. This unique dish has the flavor of a classic Southern tomato pie, but the consistency of a casserole. It doesn't get more Southern than that! The McCarty family has never revealed the exact recipe. In fact, they've never even had that angry former employee who posts the secret to the dish on social media. What follows is my best attempt at decoding it—I've gotten pretty close after years of trial and error. This is a great side dish to carry over to your next covered dish supper, or it can be eaten by itself.

In a stockpot, heat the olive oil over medium heat. Add the onion and bell pepper and cook, stirring occasionally, for 3 to 4 minutes. Add the basil, thyme, and garlic. Stir and cook until just fragrant, about 1 minute. Add the tomatoes (with the juice in the cans), salt, and black pepper. Give the mixture another quick stir, then reduce the heat to medium-low and let simmer for 30 minutes, uncovered, stirring occasionally.

Meanwhile, preheat the oven to 350°F (180°C). Once the tomato mixture has finished cooking, remove it from the heat and let cool for 5 minutes. Add the bread crumbs, Parmesan, and Cheddar. Stir the mixture until it is smooth and all the cheese has melted. Make sure there are no clumps of bread crumbs. Pour the mixture into a 13 × 9-inch (33 × 23 cm) casserole dish. Bake for 30 minutes, or until nicely browned and bubbly.

ONION PIE

5 slices bacon

4 tablespoons (55 g) salted butter

2 large yellow onions, halved
    and sliced thin

1 teaspoon sea salt

2 large eggs

½ cup (120 ml) heavy cream

1 cup (250 g) ricotta

¼ teaspoon freshly ground black pepper

1 teaspoon chopped fresh parsley

1 teaspoon flour

1 pie crust (page 177), blind baked
    per recipe instructions

Eudora Welty is part of the same Southern school of writers as William Faulkner, Flannery O'Connor, and Katherine Anne Porter—which isn't bad company! A native of Jackson, Mississippi, Eudora is an icon of Southern literature who won numerous prizes for her short stories and novels, including a Pulitzer Prize for Fiction in 1973 for The Optimist's Daughter. *What many don't know is that she was also a recipe writer. The Junior League of Jackson published a cookbook called* Southern Sideboards, *which featured an onion pie recipe from Eudora, which she credits to her friend Katherine Anne Porter. Her recipe, like many older recipes, can be a bit vague on measurements, using words like "heaping" and "a lump." However, by comparing it to recipes for the classic French dish* Tarte a l'Oignon, *I was able to fill in some of the blanks. I adapted it a little as well, adding bacon, but I still take the advice she included with the recipe: Enjoy your slice with a great glass of white wine.*

(continued)

In a heavy pot, such as a Dutch oven, fry the bacon over medium heat until it is brown and crispy, about 5 minutes. Remove the bacon from the pot and set it aside on a paper towel to cool. Crumble when cool enough to handle. Add the butter to the Dutch oven and increase the heat to medium-high. Add the onions and cook for 5 minutes, stirring occasionally to prevent burning. Reduce the heat to medium, stir in the salt, cover, and cook for 20 minutes, or until very soft. Open the lid and stir about every 5 minutes.

Note: Keep an eye on your onions! Nothing is worse than burned onions as the star of the show in this pie.

Meanwhile, preheat the oven to 400°F (200°C) and prepare the egg mixture. In a bowl, crack the eggs and beat them with a whisk until the yolks and whites are well combined. Add the heavy cream, ricotta, black pepper, parsley, crumbled bacon, and flour to the mixture and stir until just combined.

Slowly spoon the onions into the egg mixture and stir until well combined. Slowly pour the mixture into the prepared pie crust. Bake for 30 minutes, or until golden brown. Depending on your oven, you may have to rotate your pie to be sure it cooks evenly and the crust doesn't burn.

PICKLED OKRA

(pictured on page 156)

Makes 3 pints (though by all means double or triple this recipe if you have enough okra)

1 pound (455 g) fresh okra

3 cloves garlic

6 sprigs dill

1 teaspoon peppercorns

3 cups (710 ml) water

2 cups (475 ml) white vinegar

1 tablespoon (18 g) salt

1 tablespoon red pepper flakes

Folks in Mississippi, like many others across the South, love okra. In fact, if you travel to Cleveland, Mississippi, you will find Delta State University, home of the "Fighting Okra." (Officially they are the Statesmen, but students in the 1980s gave them the okra nickname and it stuck . . . now that is some serious okra love!) In the summertime, when okra is at its peak, it's easy to find pickled okra on sideboards, tables, and farmers' markets all over the Delta. This is a recipe for just such a time; it should be made and put up in the summer, then enjoyed for months.

Rinse the okra and divide it among 3 pint jars, alternating the tips up and down. Add a garlic clove and 2 dill sprigs to each jar, then divide the peppercorns evenly among each jar.

In a medium saucepan, combine the water, vinegar, and salt. Bring to a boil over medium-high heat. Add the red pepper flakes and cook for 1 minute. Carefully pour the hot liquid over the okra in the jars, leaving ½ inch (1 cm) for headroom.

To hold the okra for months, screw on the lids and process the jars per the manufacturer's instructions in a water bath or pressure canner. Store the jars in a cool, dark place. If you want to eat them quicker, you can simply store the unsealed jars in the refrigerator for up to 2 weeks.

KOOL-AID PICKLES

Makes 1 jar (32 ounces [946 ml]) of pickles

1 jar (32 ounces [946 ml]) dill pickles (spears or whole pickles)

2 packets (0.13 ounce each) unsweetened Cherry Kool-Aid

1 cup (200 g) sugar

Across the Delta, there are jars of pickles on the counters of gas stations and grocery stores. Sure, you might be thinking, "What's so special about that?" Well, I'll bet the pickles where you live aren't bright red!

While some may be put off by such a thing, I was immediately drawn to these pickles because I have a soft spot for Kool-Aid. Before you write these off as gross, give them a try! Lovers of bread-and-butter pickles in particular take quickly to the sweet-and-sour combination. The most popular flavors seem to be fruit punch or cherry, but you can experiment with other flavors. (Just don't try grape . . . trust me!) While I wish I could end this description by crediting the inventor of Kool-Aid pickles, I have thus far been unsuccessful in tracking him (or her) down. Perhaps it was just a bunch of kids with too much time on their hands in the summer. . . .

Pour all of the juice from the pickle jar into a large bowl. Add the dry Kool-Aid and sugar and stir until the Kool-Aid and sugar have completely dissolved.

If you bought spears, you can leave them in the jar. If you bought whole pickles, cut them lengthwise into spears and return them to the jar.

Pour the mixture into the jar and tighten the lid. Refrigerate for 3 days before serving.

OKRA FRIES WITH COMEBACK SAUCE

Serves 4

For the Comeback Sauce

1 cup (225 g) mayonnaise

2 tablespoons (30 g) ketchup

1 teaspoon Worcestershire sauce

¼ teaspoon freshly ground black pepper,
plus additional to taste

2 tablespoons (30 ml) hot sauce

1 teaspoon Dijon mustard

Juice of 1 lemon

½ teaspoon garlic salt

½ teaspoon onion powder

Salt to taste

For the Okra Fries

1 pound (455 g) fresh okra,
washed and cut lengthwise

3 tablespoons (45 ml) olive oil

1 teaspoon sea salt

½ teaspoon paprika

¼ teaspoon cayenne

Freshly ground black pepper to taste

In the summer okra is so abundant in the South that you may find yourself having to figure out what to do with that brown grocery bag full of okra that your neighbors just brought you because they didn't realize you just finished two 5-gallon buckets full that you had got out of your own garden. Okra fries are a great substitute for french fries on a weeknight, and they're a real crowd-pleaser. I love pairing them with Comeback Sauce, which originated in Jackson, Mississippi, at a Greek restaurant named The Rotisserie. The condiment is very close to the remoulade popular in New Orleans. It's a garlicy, creamy, mayo-based sauce that goes well with the crispy okra fries.

To make the sauce: In a mixing bowl, combine the mayonnaise, ketchup, Worcestershire sauce, black pepper, hot sauce, mustard, lemon juice, garlic salt, and onion powder. Whisk until well mixed. Add salt and additional black pepper to taste. Refrigerate the sauce until you are ready to serve. It can be held for up to a week.

To make the fries: Preheat the oven to 400°F (200°C). In a large bowl, combine the okra, olive oil, sea salt, paprika, cayenne, and black pepper. Toss until the okra is coated. Transfer the okra to a large baking sheet. If your pan isn't large enough, use two. (Make sure the okra is not stacked on top of one another, which will cause them to steam, resulting in soggy okra.) Place the pan on the middle shelf of the oven and bake for 10 minutes. Remove the pan, toss the okra with a spatula, and bake for an additional 10 minutes, or until the okra starts to brown. Serve hot with a side of Comeback Sauce.

FRIED CATFISH WITH DILL PICKLE AIOLI

Serves 6

For the Dill Pickle Aioli

½ cup (115 g) Duke's Mayonnaise
   (page 54)

3 tablespoons (25 g) chopped dill pickles

2 tablespoons finely chopped fresh dill

2 tablespoons finely chopped fresh chives

Salt to taste

Freshly ground black pepper to taste

For the Catfish

Canola oil, for frying

6 whole catfish fillets

1 cup (235 ml) buttermilk

1 cup (140 g) yellow cornmeal

½ cup (65 g) flour

2 teaspoons salt

1 tablespoon garlic powder

½ teaspoon cayenne

1 teaspoon freshly ground black pepper

The first catfish farm in the Delta was officially documented in 1965. By the end of the 1970s, Mississippi surpassed all other states in catfish farming, eventually accounting for nearly 80 percent of all the catfish production in the United States. The story of the catfish farm in the Delta is one of necessity. As global demand for common row crops such as soybeans, cotton, and wheat began to decrease, the market for these Delta staples became as inconsistent as the Delta summers. Looking for a more dependable and sustainable income, more and more farmers turned to catfish. While catfish has long been a favorite food of people of all classes in the South, the Delta was the first area to carry the Southern catfish to the next level as a sort of brand. There is just something about biting into that first piece of crispy, salty, golden brown crust of catfish and tasting that white flaky meat!

(continued)

To make the aioli: In a mixing bowl, combine the mayonnaise, pickles, dill, and chives. Mix well until the sauce is uniform. Add salt and pepper to taste. Refrigerate the aioli for 30 minutes, or until ready to serve.

To make the catfish: In a deep, heavy-bottomed pan, add canola oil until you have about 3 inches (7.5 cm) in the pan. Heat over medium until a thermometer reads 350°F to 360°F (180°C to 182°C).

While the oil comes up to temperature, place the catfish in a mixing bowl and pour the buttermilk over top. In a separate large bowl or dish, combine the cornmeal, flour, salt, garlic powder, cayenne, and black pepper. Stir to combine well.

Working in batches, thoroughly dredge the catfish fillets in the cornmeal mixture, gently shaking off any excess. Fry the fillets in the oil, avoiding crowding. Cook for 5 to 6 minutes, or until golden brown. Try to turn the fillets only once during cooking. Transfer the fillets to a paper towel to drain. Serve with the aioli.

TURNIP GREENS WITH HAM HOCKS

4 to 6 servings

2 tablespoons (28 g) butter

1 cup (160 g) diced onion

2 ham hocks (about 1 pound [455 g] each)

2 cloves garlic, minced

¼ teaspoon red pepper flakes

¼ teaspoon freshly ground black pepper

3 cups (710 ml) chicken broth

1 pound (455 g) turnip greens

On Highway 61 in Tunica, Mississippi, sits the Blue and White Restaurant. When the original location was established in 1924, it actually sat on Route 61, just a few miles away from the crossroads where legendary blues singer Robert Johnson supposedly sold his soul to the devil. No matter the address, the Blue and White has been serving up breakfast, lunch, and dinner from 5 a.m. to 10 p.m. to hungry locals for generations. Whenever my family is staying near this restaurant, we make sure to get down there when the special is Fried Chicken with Turnip Greens. These greens are inspired by the ones we eat at Blue and White, which are always flavored with ham hocks. You can certainly replicate the special by pairing them with fried chicken, but they're so flavorful you can also make a meal out of them with some cornbread on the side.

In a stockpot over medium heat, melt the butter. Add the onion and ham hocks. Cook until the onion becomes soft, about 5 minutes, stirring occasionally to prevent burning. Add the garlic, red pepper flakes, black pepper, and chicken broth. Stir the mixture and then add the turnip greens. Cover and cook for 30 minutes, stirring occasionally. Remove the ham hocks, shred the meat off the bones, and return it to the pot. Serve hot, making sure everyone gets a little meat in their turnips.

THE SOUTHERN BAKERY

Flour, Cornmeal, and Butter

Baking doesn't always come naturally—even to chefs. To this day, I'll readily admit that when I first started out in the kitchen, I wasn't a great baker. You not only have to develop a feel for it, but you also have to be very exact with measurements and cooking times. It's no wonder guests will bring a store-bought pie not only to potlucks but even to otherwise handmade holiday gatherings!

A lot of this fear is rooted in the misconception that baked goods must be perfect. Many people think that if their pie doesn't come out like the picture in the book, it won't be any good or it will be embarrassing to serve. I'm here to say: Stop worrying about perfectly crimping that pie crust. Embrace the beauty of irregular thumb indentations. It's okay if your chess pie cracked because you left it in the oven a few minutes too long (heck, as many as I bake, it still occasionally happens to me). Even if your fried skillet cornbread gets a little too brown, it will still be great eating. And people will appreciate that you took the time to stand over a hot stove to fry it for them.

I hope the recipes in this chapter will give you the confidence you need to call yourself a baker. I tried to make them straightforward enough to come out perfectly the first time. For the few that might take a little time or extra work to master (biscuits come to mind), there is no greater reward than sharing the results with your family. It turns out that baking isn't something to be afraid of as long as you take your time and cook with a heart full of love.

FRIED SKILLET CORNBREAD

Makes about 24 pieces of cornbread

1 cup (125 g) flour

1½ cups (210 g) white cornmeal

1¾ cups (410 ml) water

½ teaspoon salt

2 cups (475 ml) vegetable oil, for frying

When you think of cornbread, chances are you think of those iconic square pieces—probably baked in a glass dish. Or maybe you've discovered the beauty of cornbread cooked in a cast-iron skillet. However, I've found that most folks aren't as familiar with fried cornbread, which is traditional in many parts of the South.

I love all types of cornbread, but fried is my favorite. I have memories of walking in my grandma's door for Sunday lunch and smelling the fried cornbread. That smell could change your whole attitude for the week! A bunch of us would stand around the table before lunch was served and snap up hot pieces of cornbread as quickly as she could fry them. If you want to capture the magic, just follow the recipe below. The key to a perfect piece is the contrast between the golden brown outside and a soft, chewy inside. Once you practice with a few pieces, you'll get it down in no time.

In a mixing bowl, combine the flour, cornmeal, water, and salt and mix with a large spoon until well combined. The mixture should have the consistency of pancake batter. If the mix is too thin, add a little more cornmeal. Getting the mixture to the right texture is key! If it is too thin, it will break apart and form a thin cake.

In a 12-inch (30 cm) cast-iron skillet, add the oil, or enough of it to form a layer that is approximately ½ inch (1 cm) deep. Heat the oil over medium-high heat until it shimmers; if you have a digital instant-read thermometer, this will be about 325°F to 350°F (170°C to 180°C).

Drop in large spoonfuls of the batter. Aim for the size of a silver dollar pancake. Let each piece cook for 2 minutes, or until browned, then flip and cook for an additional 2 minutes, or until golden brown. Set aside on a paper towel and let drain while you finish cooking the remaining pieces.

BLACK PEPPER SKILLET CORNBREAD

Serves 8 to 10

1¼ cups (175 g) ground cornmeal	½ teaspoon baking soda	2 eggs, beaten
¾ cup (95 g) flour	3½ tablespoons freshly ground	6 tablespoons (85 g) butter, melted
¼ cup (50 g) sugar	black pepper	2 tablespoons (28 g) butter,
1½ teaspoons salt	⅓ cup (80 ml) heavy cream	at room temperature
2 teaspoons baking powder	1 cup (235 ml) buttermilk	

Like collards, fried chicken, and biscuits, cornbread is an iconic dish of the South. Its origins can be traced back to the American Indians, who ground down maize into a thin meal and mixed it with water and salt. As the European settlers gained a taste for cornbread, they quickly adopted it into a regular part of their diet. When commercial products such as baking powder and baking soda became more readily available to at-home cooks, cornbread evolved into a thick cakelike dish.

The flavor of this particular cornbread is unique. When most people think of the taste and texture of cornbread, they think of the crunchy texture of the outside with a salty, buttery, and almost sweet interior. This recipe brings the iconic crunch, but the inside flavor is much different. You will still get a bit of saltiness, but it's backed up by a sharp, pungent aroma from the black pepper. Pepper also adds a unique spicy heat to the cornbread. Pair it with honey for the perfect slice.

Preheat the oven to 375°F (190°C) and place a 9-inch (23 cm) cast-iron skillet in the oven to heat up as you mix your batter.

In a mixing bowl, whisk together the cornmeal, flour, sugar, salt, baking powder, baking soda, and pepper. Then add the heavy cream, buttermilk, eggs, and melted butter. Whisk together until evenly combined (it should look like a cake batter).

Using oven mitts, remove the cast-iron skillet from the oven and place on the stovetop. Carefully coat the bottom and sides with the 2 tablespoons (28 g) of room-temperature butter, making sure the pan is well greased. Pour the batter into the skillet and place it in the oven.

Bake until the center is firm or until a toothpick inserted into the center comes out clean, about 20 minutes. Allow to cool before serving.

BENNE SEED CHEDDAR DROP BISCUITS

Makes about 20 small biscuits

2 cups (250 g) flour

2 teaspoons baking powder

1 teaspoon salt

½ cup (1 stick, 112 g) unsalted butter, cut into ¼-inch (0.5 cm) pieces

½ cup (58 g) shredded Cheddar cheese

½ cup (72 g) benne seeds

¾ cup (175 ml) cold whole milk

Benne *is the West African word for sesame. Benne seeds were brought to the American South by West African slaves, along with Carolina Gold rice and red peas (two more well-known imports). Benne seeds made their first appearance in the Low Country of South Carolina in the early 1700s. As benne seeds grew in popularity, they were commercially farmed for uses such as cooking oil. Eventually, other crops proved to be more profitable, and the benne seed was grown in limited quantities until its near disappearance in the late 19th century.*

Though true benne seeds almost went extinct, thanks to people such as Glenn Roberts of Anson Mills, you can now order heirloom benne seeds. It's worth giving them a try! While these biscuits taste just fine with regular sesame seeds, for the full experience you'll want the unique, almost bitter flavor of the heirloom benne seeds.

Preheat the oven to 350°F (180°C). Line a baking sheet with parchment paper or grease a sheet pan with butter.

In a mixing bowl, whisk together the flour, baking powder, and salt. Add the butter and blend with a pastry cutter or a fork. Work the butter and dry ingredients together until the butter is well blended and the mixture resembles coarse cornmeal.

Add the cheese and benne seeds. Slowly add the milk and mix with a fork until the dough becomes slightly sticky. Scoop the dough out with a tablespoon onto the parchment paper, leaving space for the biscuits to expand. (If you want to make larger biscuits, you can use an ice cream scoop instead.)

Bake for 10 minutes, or until golden brown. Serve warm or at room temperature.

SWEET BUTTERMILK BISCUITS WITH STRAWBERRIES

Serves 10

1½ pounds (680 g) strawberries, stemmed and quartered

¾ cup (150 g) sugar, divided

2 cups (250 g) flour

¼ teaspoon baking soda

1 tablespoon baking powder

½ cup (1 stick, 112 g) cold unsalted butter, cut into small pieces and refrigerated (see note)

1 cup (235 ml) low-fat buttermilk

One afternoon I was visiting with my dear friend Gene Hammer from the legendary restaurant Crook's Corner, and our conversation turned to biscuits. Gene mentioned that before his passing, renowned chef Bill Neal used to make a sweet biscuit and turn it into strawberry shortcake. That's all it took for me to dive elbow-deep into a bag of flour! The sweetness of these biscuits actually works well with the tartness that comes from the buttermilk. When you pile fresh strawberries on them, the biscuits are transformed into a savory dessert. Unfortunately, I never had a chance to taste Bill Neal's sweet biscuits . . . I'll just have to pray that he would approve!

Preheat the oven to 350°F (180°C). Grease a baking sheet and set aside.

In a mixing bowl, stir the strawberries and ¼ cup (50 g) of the sugar together. Refrigerate for at least 30 minutes (or long enough for the juice to run from the strawberries).

In a separate mixing bowl, sift together the flour, remaining ½ cup sugar (100 g), baking soda, and baking powder. Stir to combine.

Remove the butter from the refrigerator or freezer and use a pastry cutter or knife to blend it with the dry ingredients. Blend until the mixture resembles crumbs or small peas (there will still be small pieces of butter). (While it might be tempting, don't use your hands to mix the butter into the dough. The heat from your hands will warm up the butter, which will alter your results.)

Working quickly, make a hole in the middle of the mixture and add the buttermilk. Mix with a spatula until the mixture is well combined, then pour the mixture onto a floured surface.

Using a rolling pin, roll the mixture into a square that's about 2 inches (5 cm) thick. If you need to firm up the edges, you can use a refrigerated kitchen knife.

(continued)

KEEPING IT COLD

If you've made biscuits before, then you know how easy it is to get obsessed with "the perfect biscuit." Different chefs abide by different rules—and sometimes superstitions. My own experience has told me that the most important part of a batch of biscuits is keeping the butter cold up until the moment you bake.

This means that as I work through the recipe, I stress about keeping the butter cold. If you'd like to do the same, I recommend going to the extreme. Before you get started, refrigerate your mixing bowl, a few extra knives, and any other tools that will touch the dough. Don't use your hands to mix the butter into the dough, and expose the mixture to heat as little as possible.

If you manage to keep the butter cold enough, I'm confident you'll turn out biscuits that are fluffy inside with a crispy outside!

Cut the dough into 4 equal parts and stack them on top of each other. Then roll the dough out again with the rolling pin until the mixture is about 1½ inches (3.5 cm) thick.

Cut out about 10 squares, or squares in your desired size. Transfer the pieces to the baking sheet and bake for 12 to 15 minutes, or until golden brown.

Remove the strawberry mixture from the refrigerator. When the biscuits have cooled slightly, remove them from the pan and slice each one in half horizontally. Plate each biscuit so that it's open-faced and spoon some strawberries and juice over one side. Close the biscuit and spoon more strawberries over the top.

Note: Cut the butter into small pieces and place in the refrigerator or freezer while you measure out all of the dry ingredients. You want the butter to be as cold as possible without being frozen.

PIE CRUST

Makes 1 pie crust

1½ cups (190 g) flour

½ teaspoon salt

3 tablespoons (38 g) vegetable shortening,
   such as Crisco

5 tablespoons (70 g) cold, unsalted butter,
   cut into ¼-inch (0.5 cm) cubes

6 to 8 tablespoons (90 to 120 ml)
   ice-cold water

Pie crust can be finicky, like many other elements of baking. This recipe is one I've settled on over the years because I find it to be both easier than most pie crusts yet also quite reliable. I know I'm not perfectly consistent, yet it produces a buttery, flaky crust every time. This pie crust can be made a few days ahead and stored in the refrigerator until you're ready to use it. You can also make a few and freeze them once they're rolled out and laid flat.

In a mixing bowl, whisk together the flour and salt. Add the shortening, working it in with a pastry cutter or by hand until the mixture is combined but crumbly.

Add the butter to the flour mixture, working it in with a pastry cutter or by hand. Don't stress out if the mixture isn't evenly mixed; you should have big and small chunks of butter in the mixture.

Add 3 tablespoons of the water and mix with a fork until well combined. Gradually add additional water to the mixture until it becomes chunky. The goal is a dough that will barely hold together if you squeeze it.

Scoop the mixture out of the bowl and onto a piece of parchment paper. Flatten it out a bit by hand. If there are dry parts of the dough, add a small amount of water to your hands and wipe it over the top of the dry areas. Try not to overwet the dough.

Fold the dough over on itself from left to right, then top to bottom. Through this process the dry crumbs will begin to incorporate themselves into the dough. If there are still parts of the dough that appear to be dry, add a small amount of water by hand. Repeat the folding process several times until all of the crumbs are combined and the dough is fully formed with a claylike consistency.

(continued)

Shape the dough into a disk about 1 inch (2.5 cm) thick, wrap it in plastic wrap, and place it in the refrigerator for 45 minutes. About 10 to 15 minutes before you are ready to roll your pie crust, remove it from the refrigerator and let it rest at room temperature to allow the butter to soften.

Roll the pie dough out with a rolling pin, keeping it on the parchment paper. Cut the dough to the desired size. In this book, we'll use a 12-inch (30 cm) round of dough for a 9-inch (23 cm) pie. Transfer the dough to the pie pan, then place it back in the refrigerator while you prepare your pie recipe (see pages 181 to 197) or proceed to the next step.

For the recipes in this book, and most likely for any of your own recipes, you'll want to blind bake the pie shell before filling it. To do this, preheat your oven to 450°F (230°C). Make a few small pricks in the bottom and sides of the dough with a fork. Use pastry weights or fill the bottom of the pie with dry beans. Bake the pie shell for 5 minutes. Let it cool to room temperature before using with one of the recipes that follows.

CHOCOLATE CHESS PIE WITH PECANS

Makes one 9-inch (23 cm) pie

1½ cups (300 g) sugar

5 tablespoons (27 g) unsweetened
   cocoa powder

½ teaspoon ground black coffee

⅓ cup (75 g) butter, melted

2 tablespoons (15 g) flour

3 eggs, beaten

½ cup (120 ml) condensed milk

¼ teaspoon vanilla extract

1½ cups (150 g) chopped pecans

1 Pie Crust (page 177), blind baked
   per recipe instructions

Ice cream, for serving

Chess Pie is often presented as a classic Southern pie . . . but is it? The ingredients and techniques can actually be traced back to England. On the one hand, I've found similar recipes in books from the mid-1700s, like Martha Washington's Booke of Cookery. *However, I've also found there is a legend that places its origins firmly in the South. Folklore says that the recipe came from a plantation cook who had to make up a pie using only ingredients that would have been readily available at hand. When she was asked what type of pie she made, her reply was "just pie." In a deep Southern accent, this sounded like "chess pie." Having a very pronounced Southern accent myself, I tend to like this story the best.*

No matter where the name came from, Chess Pie has become a classic Southern pie in the decades since. The recipe is very adaptable, as it can transform flavors with the simplest of ingredient additions. My personal favorite is chocolate: You'll find the deep richness of this pie complemented with just a hint of coffee really takes it to a new level.

Preheat the oven to 375°F (190°C).

In a mixing bowl, combine the sugar, cocoa, coffee, and melted butter and stir until mixed. In a separate mixing bowl, combine the flour, eggs, condensed milk, and vanilla and stir.

Pour the flour mixture into the sugar mixture. Add the pecans and stir until the mixture is uniform.

Pour into the blind-baked pie crust. Bake for 10 minutes, then reduce the heat to 325°F (170°C) and bake for an additional 30 minutes, or until the pie is set.

Let the pie cool to room temperature. Serve with ice cream.

SWEET POTATO PIE

Makes one 9-inch (23 cm) pie

3 small sweet potatoes, or enough for
    about 2 cups (450 g) mashed potatoes

2 eggs

4 tablespoons (55 g) butter, melted

¾ cup (150 g) sugar

½ cup (120 ml) heavy cream

½ teaspoon vanilla extract

1 teaspoon ground cinnamon

1 Pie Crust (page 177), blind baked
    per recipe instructions

In my part of the state, it's not hard to find a sweet potato field. I guess it's no surprise that we eat more sweet potato pie than pumpkin pie around here. But how did the sweet potato pie become a staple throughout the South?

During the early 16th century, European settlers introduced the pumpkin pie to West African tribes. As people grew to enjoy the taste of the sweet pumpkin pie, they wanted to create a pie of their own. Because pumpkin isn't grown in West Africa, naturally they turned to sweet potatoes and yams, which were grown in abundance. As these crops were brought to the United States, the sweet potato pie migrated with them and was soon on tables across the South. Although pumpkin pie and sweet potato pie are close cousins, I prefer the warm fall flavors and chunky consistency of a sweet potato pie like this one.

Preheat the oven to 400°F (200°C). Roast the sweet potatoes until they are soft when pierced with a fork, about 45 minutes. Remove from the oven and let them cool.

Reduce the oven temperature to 350°F (180°C). Remove the skins from the potatoes and discard. In a mixing bowl, mash the sweet potatoes with a potato masher or fork. Measure to make sure you have about 2 cups of potatoes. Remove any extra potato mash from the bowl.

Add the eggs to the sweet potatoes and stir to combine. Add the melted butter, sugar, heavy cream, vanilla, and cinnamon and stir until well combined.

Pour the mixture into the blind-baked pie crust. Bake for 35 minutes, or until the filling has set. Let cool to room temperature.

BUTTERMILK PIE

Makes one 9-inch (23 cm) pie

3 eggs

1½ cups (300 g) sugar

3 tablespoons (42 g) butter, melted

2 tablespoons (15 g) flour

1 cup (235 ml) buttermilk

1 tablespoon grated lemon zest

⅛ teaspoon ground nutmeg

1 teaspoon vanilla extract

1 Pie Crust (page 177), blind baked
   per recipe instructions

Buttermilk pie was brought to the South by English settlers. Although similar in texture to chess pie (see page 181), the original recipes for these two pies are different. For chess pie, the flour, butter, sugar, and eggs were the main ingredients and were often stabilized with cornmeal. However, in the original buttermilk pie recipes, sugar, eggs, and buttermilk were the main ingredients. As recipes evolved over decades of baking, the similarities won out—for example, milk (though not buttermilk) was eventually added to the original recipe for chess pie. Also like chess pie, buttermilk pie's rise to popularity was out of necessity. When fresh fruit wasn't in season, this was a flavorful pie that was easy to make with things that are always in the pantry (sugar, flour, buttermilk, and eggs). Enjoy the sweet and tangy pie with a cup of coffee to cut through the sweetness.

Preheat the oven to 350°F (180°C).

In a mixing bowl, combine the eggs and sugar, stirring together until well combined. Stir in the melted butter, flour, buttermilk, lemon zest, nutmeg, and vanilla. Mix until smooth.

Pour the mixture into the blind-baked pie crust. Bake for 40 minutes, or until the pie has set—it should have a slight jiggle.

Let the pie cool to room temperature before serving.

COCONUT CREAM PIE

Makes one 9-inch (23 cm) pie

For the Pie

2 cups (475 ml) heavy cream

2 eggs

¾ cup (150 g) sugar

¼ cup (32 g) cornstarch

1 teaspoon vanilla extract

1 teaspoon coconut extract

1½ cups (125 g) shredded
   dried coconut, divided

1 Pie Crust (page 177), fully baked
   for 10 minutes

For the Whipped Cream Topping

1½ cups (355 ml) heavy cream

¼ cup (50 g) sugar

1 teaspoon vanilla extract

In the early 1800s Americans fell in love with tropical fruits like bananas and pineapples, but not coconut. The problem at the time was that it was hard to transport coconuts fresh—most arrived spoiled, or at the very least, not as delicious as they should be. In the late 1800s that all changed when a Philadelphia flour miller quickly dried and shredded coconut meat to preserve it, in the process creating a new way to deliver coconut as a more shelf-stable product. As coconut spread, recipes like coconut cream pie began showing up in cookbooks in the early 1900s.

Preheat the oven to 350°F (180°C).

To make the pie: In a medium saucepan, combine the heavy cream and eggs and stir well. Cook over medium heat until the mixture is warm. Add the sugar and cornstarch and continue cooking, whisking frequently, until the mixture thickens, about 5 minutes.

Remove the pan from the heat and stir in the vanilla extract, coconut extract, and 1 cup (85 g) of the coconut. Pour the mixture into the fully baked pie crust and place the pie in the refrigerator until cold, about 1 hour.

Place the remaining ½ cup (40 g) coconut on a baking sheet and bake until golden brown, about 2 to 4 minutes. Cool on the baking sheet.

To make the whipped cream topping: In a stand mixer or with a hand mixer, whip together the heavy cream, sugar, and vanilla at medium speed until the mixture is light and fluffy. If your pie is not yet done cooling, place the whipped cream in the refrigerator.

Remove the chilled pie from the refrigerator, spread the whipped cream evenly on top of the pie, and garnish the top with the toasted coconut. When you are finished, return the pie to the refrigerator until you are ready to serve it. This pie should always be served chilled.

COCONUT PIE

Makes one 9-inch (23 cm) pie

1 cup (235 ml) milk

½ cup (120 ml) sweetened
   condensed milk

1 cup (200 g) sugar

1 cup (85 g) shredded dried coconut

2 eggs, beaten

3 tablespoons (25 g) flour

1 tablespoon (14 g) butter, melted

1 teaspoon vanilla extract

2 tablespoons (30 ml) dark rum
   (such as Myers)

1 Pie Crust (page 177), blind baked
   per recipe instructions

While you might think the previous recipe for coconut cream pie is all a coconut lover would ever need, I'm here to tell you that it's okay to see other pies. While the previous pie is a cool classic, this coconut pie is punched up with rum and served warm. The boozy addition helps balance the rich, creamy coconut and makes this pie a fall or winter stunner. My favorite bite is when this pie is still hot—cooled just enough so that it doesn't scald the roof of my mouth.

Preheat the oven to 350°F (180°C).

In a mixing bowl, combine the milk, condensed milk, sugar, coconut, eggs, flour, melted butter, vanilla, and rum. Stir until you have a uniform mixture.

Pour the mixture into the blind-baked pie shell. Bake for 40 minutes, or until a toothpick or knife inserted near the center comes out clean. Depending on your oven, you may have to rotate the pie during baking to make sure it browns evenly.

Let the pie cool to room temperature before serving.

PEANUT PIE

Makes one 9-inch (23 cm) pie

2 eggs

⅓ cup (65 g) sugar

⅓ cup (80 ml) light corn syrup

⅓ cup (80 ml) dark corn syrup

4 tablespoons (55 g) butter, melted

¼ teaspoon vanilla extract

¼ teaspoon sea salt

1 cup (145 g) salted peanuts

1 Pie Crust (page 177), blind baked
   per recipe instructions

Whipped cream or ice cream, for serving

I've done plenty of digging, but I still can't puzzle out the exact origin of this recipe. The closest I've come is tracing back peanut's introduction into the South from West African slaves. Since peanuts were once considered a lowly food, that sheds light on the alternate name for this recipe: Poor Man's Pecan Pie.

Unlike peanut butter pie, which is made with whipped cream and peanut butter, refrigerated overnight, and then served cold, peanut pie is baked. Its flavors are also more concentrated on the salty peanut itself. Try rolling it out at your next gathering and impress your friends with a pie that packs the true flavor of peanuts.

Preheat the oven to 350°F (180°C).

In a mixing bowl, combine the eggs, sugar, light and dark corn syrups, butter, vanilla, and salt. Stir until evenly combined.

Fold in the peanuts, then pour the mixture into the blind-baked pie crust. Bake for 35 minutes, or until the pie is golden brown.

Let the pie cool to room temperature and serve with whipped cream or a big scoop of ice cream.

PECAN PIE BREAD PUDDING

Serves about 16

1 loaf (16 ounces [455 g]) French bread
  (stale bread is key)

5 eggs

1 cup (200 g) granulated sugar

1½ cups (340 g) packed brown sugar

1 cup (235 ml) heavy cream

2 cups (475 ml) milk

1 cup (235 ml) dark corn syrup

2 tablespoons (30 ml) vanilla extract

1 cup (110 g) chopped pecans, divided

Ice cream, for serving

Bread pudding has been around for centuries, with variations that are popular all over the world. I've traced its origins all the way back to the ancient Romans! In America, bread pudding has been around since colonial times and was a very popular dish in the 18th century. In Hannah Glasse's 1747 cookbook, The Art of Cookery Made Plain and Easy, *there are three different variations on bread pudding recipes. Also, in Thomas Jefferson's recipe notes you will find a couple of sauce recipes that are for bread pudding (they likely came from his love for classic French cooking). It has also been documented that Jefferson had a daily bread delivery to Monticello of three baguettes. I'm pretty sure when all the bread was not used during the day, a bread pudding would be expected for dessert. This recipe riffs on the original by combining it with the ingredients of classic Southern pecan pie. The pecans add an extra crunch to the light and fluffy bread pudding.*

Preheat the oven to 350°F (180°C). Grease an 8 × 8-inch (20 × 20 cm) baking pan.

Cube or tear the bread into 1½-inch (3.5 cm) pieces and place them in a mixing bowl. In a separate mixing bowl, add the eggs, granulated sugar, brown sugar, heavy cream, milk, dark corn syrup, and vanilla and stir to combine. Fold in ½ cup (55 g) of the pecans.

Pour the liquid mixture over the bread. Use your hands or a large spoon to ensure you soak every piece of bread.

Transfer the mixture to the baking pan, making sure all of the liquid makes it into the pan. Top the bread pudding with the remaining ½ cup (55 g) pecans.

Bake for 35 minutes, or until most of the pudding is set and the middle is still a little jiggly.

Allow to cool for 20 minutes. Serve while still warm, with a scoop of ice cream. Refrigerate any leftovers and reheat as you'd like. This also makes for a delicious sweet breakfast, paired with a cup of coffee.

THE MELVIN GIRLS' LEMON BLUEBERRY PIE

Makes one 9-inch (23 cm) pie

2 teaspoons grated lemon zest	1 cup (145 g) fresh blueberries	½ teaspoon cream of tartar
2 eggs, separated	½ cup (120 ml) lemon juice	¼ cup (50 g) sugar
1 can (14 ounces [397 g]) sweetened condensed milk	1 Pie Crust (page 177), blind baked per recipe instructions	

My dad has been a pastor at the same small Baptist church for more than three decades. Naturally, because I grew up in that church, many members ended up feeling like extended family to me. Sisters Betty Sanderson and Lela Harrell in particular were like grandmothers to me. In 1999, along with their two other sisters, they published a small spiral-bound cookbook called Family and Food by the Melvin Sisters. *To this day, that book is a valuable resource for regional Southern recipes when I'm looking for inspiration.*

This pie is one of my family's favorite recipes from that book. While I tinker with just about every recipe, sometimes you just can't mess with perfection. (Plus, my wife would not be happy if I messed with the recipe for her favorite pie.) My only advice is to make this pie with fresh blueberries, ideally when they are at their peak in summer.

Preheat the oven to 325°F (170°C).

In a mixing bowl, combine the lemon zest with the egg yolks, condensed milk, blueberries, and lemon juice. Stir just until the mixture thickens, then pour into the blind-baked pie crust and set aside.

To make the meringue, combine the egg whites and cream of tartar in the bowl of a stand mixer or a separate mixing bowl and beat over medium speed until the mixture becomes stiff. Add the sugar, pouring it in gradually while the mixer continues to beat the egg whites. Continue to beat until the mixture begins to form stiff peaks.

Spoon the meringue on top of the pie, spreading it evenly and piling it as high as you can get it. Bake the pie until lightly browned on top, about 8 minutes.

Let the pie cool to room temperature, or at least for an hour, before slicing and serving.

CHOCOLATE FUDGE AND SEA SALT PIE

Makes one 9-inch (23 cm) pie

¾ cup (170 g) butter

¾ cup (130 g) semisweet
   chocolate morsels

2 eggs

½ cup (100 g) sugar

3 tablespoons (25 g) flour

1 teaspoon vanilla extract

1½ tablespoons (27 g) sea salt, divided

¼ cup (60 ml) heavy cream

1 Pie Crust (page 177), blind baked
   per recipe instructions

Vanilla ice cream, for serving

I come from a family that loves chocolate—I mean really loves the stuff. When you go with us to a family reunion, the dessert table will be full of all kinds of pies and cakes—nearly all with some form of chocolate. Because there is nothing worse than driving to a family reunion thinking about chocolate pie only to have it disappear before you get your slice, I eventually had to learn to make my own. In this pie, I added fresh sea salt from our friends at Sea Love Sea Salt Co. to cut through the richness of the fudge. This is definitely a pie for those who love the intersection of sweet and salty.

Preheat the oven to 325°F (170°C).

Add water to a double boiler and place on the stove over medium heat. Once it's warm, add the butter and chocolate morsels to the upper bowl of the boiler.

While your butter and chocolate begin to melt, beat the eggs in a mixing bowl. Add the sugar, flour, vanilla, and ½ tablespoon (9 g) sea salt to the eggs and mix until well combined.

When the butter and chocolate are almost fully melted, add the heavy cream and stir until the mixture is completely combined and smooth.

Fold the chocolate mixture into the egg mixture and stir together until well combined.

Pour the mixture into the blind-baked pie crust and bake for 25 to 30 minutes, or until the pie has set (it should still have a slight jiggle).

After the pie has cooled to room temperature, sprinkle the remaining 1 tablespoon (18 g) sea salt evenly across the top of the pie. Serve each slice with a scoop of vanilla ice cream.

SOUTHERN SUPPER MENUS

At my restaurant in Garland, North Carolina, we host a dinner series a few times a year called the South Supper Series. The concept comes from old Southern supper clubs, where family and friends would meet for food and fellowship. It was important to have people from different places and walks of life gather around large community tables and enjoy one another's company over a plate of food. These dinners are often themed by certain regions across the South. On the following pages, you'll find similar themed dinners that just might make your next dinner party a bit easier by providing a theme, menu, and even some music suggestions to help make it a great event. Enjoy!

EASTERN NORTH CAROLINA PIG PICKIN'

If you want to throw a barbecue party, this should be your go-to menu. You can change it up and use the western-style sauce and slaw (pages 45 and 66) or make both for an east versus west showdown. This should be eaten outside with paper plates . . . nothing fancy here!

SMOKED BOSTON BUTT WITH EASTERN NORTH CAROLINA VINEGAR SAUCE (PAGE 42)

EASTERN NORTH CAROLINA WHITE SLAW (PAGE 65)

FRIED SKILLET CORNBREAD (PAGE 168)

BBQ POTATOES (PAGE 78)

MAC AND CHEESE (PAGE 69)

SWEET BUTTERMILK BISCUITS WITH STRAWBERRIES (PAGE 175)

If the weather is cool, a pot of Brunswick "Georgia" Stew (page 111) will also go very nicely with this menu.

I love live music when you are having a party outside, so I am going to recommend two live albums from North Carolina bands that are in our rotation a lot: James Taylor's *Live* and the Avett Brothers' *Live, Volume 3*. Mixing in a little bit of Carolina beach music won't hurt either; try out General Johnson and Chairman of the Board.

SURF AND TURF CAROLINA STYLE

If you are looking for something a little more upscale, this menu is just for you. Get out the fine china and make sure the sideboard has been dusted. Normally some type of potato is served with beef, but for this menu I used Squash and Rice Pudding as the starch. It's also beautiful on the plate.

COLLARD CHOWDER (PAGE 60)

COFFEE-RUBBED WHOLE BEEF TENDERLOIN (PAGE 145)

SALTINE CRACKER FRIED OYSTERS (PAGE 55)

SQUASH AND RICE PUDDING (PAGE 70)

CHOCOLATE FUDGE AND SEA SALT PIE (PAGE 197)

For this dinner party, I would go with the classic sounds of North Carolina native Nina Simone. Try the 1965 classic *I Put a Spell on You*.

LOW COUNTRY BOIL

A Low Country boil can be enjoyed anytime of year, but I recommend aiming for the summer when fresh shrimp are abundant. Eat it outside under a big tree, gathered around a huge community table.

FROGMORE STEW, A.K.A. THE LOW COUNTRY BOIL (PAGE 104)

SHRIMP AND OKRA (PAGE 100)

FUNERAL GRITS (PAGE 113)

COCONUT CREAM PIE (PAGE 186)

Try any of these bands for an outside Low Country–themed party: Blue Dogs' *Live at the Dock Street Theatre*, the Drive-By Truckers' *This Weekend's the Night!* and almost anything from Hootie and the Blowfish.

A JUKE JOINT SATURDAY NIGHT

This was one of my favorites when we did it at the restaurant. First, a warning: The menu will probably be the most time-consuming of all the menus I'm recommending in this section. However, with some careful planning, you will pull it off without a hitch . . . and I can guarantee you people will talk about it for years to come!

MEMPHIS DRY-RUB RIBS (PAGE 124)

FRIED CATFISH WITH DILL PICKLE AIOLI (PAGE 161)

DELTA TAMALES (PAGE 129)

STIR-FRIED COLLARDS WITH SPICY TOMATO CHOW-CHOW (PAGE 147)

MERIGOLD TOMATOES (PAGE 151)

FRIED SKILLET CORNBREAD (PAGE 168)

CHOCOLATE CHESS PIE WITH PECANS (PAGE 181)

As for music, a playlist doesn't get much better than this: Start with B.B. King, then move on to John Lee Hooker, Muddy Waters, and Howlin' Wolf. As the night goes on, don't forget about guys like Mississippi John Hurt, Lead Belly, and Lightnin' Hopkins. Last but not least, work in some Robert Johnson.

MY SOUTH

This is a menu of my personal favorites. If I was preparing a last meal for myself, it would look a lot like this.

BUTTERMILK FRIED CHICKEN (PAGE 49)

SMOKED SHRIMP (PAGE 99)

LENOIR COUNTY FISH STEW (PAGE 63)

RED RICE (PAGE 117)

PORK BELLY AND SWEET POTATO HASH (PAGE 74)

TURNIP GREENS WITH HAM HOCKS (PAGE 164)

COCONUT PIE (PAGE 189)

SWEET POTATO PIE (PAGE 182)

My playlist would have to be *The Essential Sam Cooke*.

THE SOUTHERN PANTRY

Top shelf starting on the left. The bottom shelf begins with Duke's Mayonnaise.

Shawnee Flour: This flour has been a constant in our family. The texture is a bit different from most store-bought flours; it is much finer and has a light feel to it.

Lundy's Lard: Many commercially bought lards contain lard and hydrogenated lard. However, Lundy's lard contains only refined lard, which just means it has been filtered to get the small bits out. It adds fluffiness to things like tamales and biscuits.

Geechie Boy Mill Grits: At Geechie Boy Mill, heirloom corn is ground down in antique grist-mills, which preserves the natural oils and flavors in the corn. The result is the best-tasting grits you'll ever have.

Buffaloe Milling Company Corn Meal: A North Carolina staple for more than 100 years. I don't think I have ever made a piece of cornbread without using it. I love the sweetness that comes from this specific mill.

Duke's Mayonnaise: Throughout the book I recommend Duke's, as I believe the creamy, salty flavor makes this mayo a step above the rest. It can liven up anything from slaw to chicken salad.

Anson Mills Carolina Gold Rice: A very clean and sweet-flavored rice, Carolina Gold is extremely delicate and has a very distinct flavor.

It is also versatile: It can be used to make fluffy rice, sticky rice, and even risotto.

Sea Love Sea Salt Co. Sea Salt: I have used all kinds of sea salt, but the richest flavors I have ever tasted come from Sea Love Sea Salt. The procedure they use is what makes it so unique and flavorful. It is harvested from the waters off North Carolina and then left to dry naturally in green-houses using only solar energy. They do a great job of preserving the natural flavors in the salt.

Anson Mills Benne Seeds: Benne seeds have a unique nuttiness to them that you just can't find in modern sesame seeds. They add an extra layer of flavor to any dish.

Texas Pete Hot Sauce: This classic hot sauce has a great balance of heat and salt. I love that it isn't overly peppery. You will be hard-pressed to find any barbecue places in the state of North Carolina that don't have at least one or two bottles floating around their dining room.

Piggly Wiggly Mustard: No need to get fancy with mustard. I find that the vinegary acidity of this store-brand mustard goes well with most recipes.

Dixie Crystals Sugar: Since 1917, Dixie Crystals has been producing quality cane sugar. I find it dissolves much more quickly than most other sugars.

A FEW BOOKS

Here are a few books that I love about barbecue, food, and food history in the South:

Holy Smoke: The Big Book of North Carolina Barbecue, by John Shelton Reed and Dale Volberg Reed, with William McKinney. This is a book that changed everything for me and the way I cook barbecue.

Barbecue, by John Shelton Reed. A fine recipe book celebrating all types of Southern barbecue.

Deep Run Roots: Stories and Recipes from My Corner of the South, by Vivian Howard. This is a great Southern cookbook written by one of the leading chefs in North Carolina and the South.

Franklin Barbecue: A Meat-Smoking Manifesto, by Aaron Franklin and Jordan Mackay. James Beard Award–winning pit master Aaron Franklin explores the ins and outs of his style of barbecue—a must-have for every barbecue bookshelf.

Root to Leaf: A Southern Chef Cooks through the Seasons, by Steven Satterfield. A seasonal cookbook that explores the bounties found in your garden or local farmers' market.

Seasoned in the South: Recipes from Crook's Corner and from Home, by Bill Smith. Classic Southern recipes told and explained in a way that only Bill Smith can tell them. A must-have for any Southern kitchen.

The Taste of Country Cooking, by Edna Lewis. A true Southern classic by the groundbreaking chef Edna Lewis.

High on the Hog: A Culinary Journey from Africa to America, by Jessica B. Harris. A beautifully told story about the influence of African Americans on Southern cuisine and its history.

The Edible South: The Power of Food and the Making of an American Region, by Marcie Cohen Ferris. A great book on how food has shaped the South that we know.

To Live and Dine in Dixie: The Evolution of Urban Food Culture in the Jim Crow South, by Angela Jill Cooley. This book explores food culture as it changed during the Jim Crow era.

Eat Drink Delta: A Hungry Traveler's Journey through the Soul of the South, by Susan Puckett. This is a comprehensive guide to eating your way through the Mississippi Delta.

THANK YOU

Embarking on a project as hard as writing a book truly takes a great team of people. First off, I have to thank my editor, Thom O'Hearn, and the entire team at Quarto. I thought I had an idea of what it took to write a book, but I didn't. I will forever be grateful for Thom, walking me through this project, dealing with my bad grammar, and helping make this book what it is. Thank you for always answering the phone when I called in a panic or was completely overwhelmed with this. I couldn't have asked for a better editor.

A very important part of a book is the photography. Thank you, Felicia Perry Trujillo, Susan Johnson Smith, and Forrest Mason, for taking a vision that was in my head and turning it into amazing photos. The work and dedication you put into taking these photos is something I will forever be grateful for. Also thank you, Replacements Limited, for providing us with an array of dish options that helped the vision become complete.

One of the most important things to me as a chef is the fresh ingredients I have access to. I want to thank four people who provide us with the best products we could ask for: Esther Ivey of Heritage Farms Cheshire Pork, Jimmy Burch of Burch Farms, Billy Augustine of Pretty Boy Farms, and Amanda Jacobs of Sea Love Sea Salt. I am a believer that without great farmers, you can't have great food.

I have had so many friends and chefs who have played a crucial role in what I do. Johnathan Grady and Jason Barefoot, thanks for sitting up all those nights when we were just getting started. Jason Frye, thanks for always being a great sounding board to bounce ideas off of, and for helping me through writer's block! Jennifer Rice, thanks for falling in love with Squash and Rice Pudding and a little barbecue place in eastern North Carolina. To my Wilmington guys, Keith Rhodes, Dean Neff, and Craig Love, thank you for being supporters, and friends, from the beginning. I am thankful to call guys like Harrison Sapp, Griffin Bufkin, Aaron Siegel, Taylor Garrigan, Madison Ruckel, Anthony Dibernardo, Michael Letchworth, Sam Jones, Elliott Moss, Bryan Furman, and so many more who are part of my barbecue family. To Bill Smith, I never thought when I started this culinary journey that my path would cross with yours or that I would step in the hallowed halls of Crook's Corner's kitchen and be able to stand in that very kitchen and cook. The wisdom and guidance that you have shared with me is something I am grateful for every day.

To my employees, or as I like to refer to them, "my SSBBQ kids," you guys don't get enough credit for the success of our business. Each one of you has bought into our core beliefs and has carried our vision to places I never would have dreamed it would go. To Rodolfo Sandoval, I couldn't ask for a better person to be at my side every day in the kitchen. You give me everything you have every day. Evan Salzano, thank you for your behind the scenes work on this project and everything else I set out on—you are truly the little brother I never had. I am happy to call you family.

Thank you to my parents, Tim and Lynn Register, for always being supportive in whatever path I have decided to go down. Your love and support are something I will never be able to repay. Most important, thank you for showing me the value and importance of sitting down every night at the dinner table with the people you love the most.

To my children, Taylor Grace, Nash, and Harrison, I hope the traditions and meals we share together, which may seem trivial now, will give you a lifetime of laughs, memories, and full bellies. Thanks for dealing with me constantly talking about this book. Each one of you inspires me to be better every day, but most important, you make me a better person.

To my wife, Jessica, I am so thankful that I get to walk hand in hand with you through this crazy journey we call life. You have supported me through every aspect of our life together, even when it meant putting your dreams and aspirations on the back burner. You have seen me at my very best and my very worst, but always offer me unconditional support and love. You are my muse, my best friend, and undoubtedly my rock: Without you, I wouldn't be who I am today. Thank you, my love.

ABOUT THE AUTHOR

Chef Matthew Register and his wife Jessica own Southern Smoke BBQ, which has been featured in *Food & Wine* magazine and on the *Today Show*, and was named one of the top 25 BBQ restaurants in the United States by *Men's Journal*. They also own South Catering and the Southern Smoke BBQ food truck. Matthew has always had a passion for fine food and the outdoors, and he prides himself on incorporating fresh, local ingredients. Raised in rural eastern North Carolina, he grew up in a community that formed inseparable bonds through deep-rooted traditions at the dinner table. These traditions are ones that he hopes to sustain, not just for his three young children, but for his community and those who dine with him as well.

INDEX